YOU CAN RAISE
A WELL-
MANNERED
CHILD

YOU CAN RAISE
A WELL-
MANNERED
CHILD

🍂 MEETING AND GREETING 🍂 GOING OUT

IN PUBLIC 🍂 TELEPHONE CONVERSATIONS

🍂 TABLE MANNERS 🍂 AND MUCH MORE

June Hines Moore

BROADMAN
& HOLMAN
PUBLISHERS

Nashville, Tennessee

© 1996
by June Hines Moore
All rights reserved
Printed in the United States of America

Published by:
Broadman & Holman Publishers
Nashville, Tennessee
4260-76
0-8054-6076-4

Acquisitions and Development Editor: Janis Whipple
Interior Design & Production: Desktop Miracles, Inc.

Dewey Decimal Classification: 649
Subject Heading: CHILDREARING / COURTESY
Library of Congress Card Catalog Number: 96-13111

All names have been changed. Unless otherwise indicated, all Scripture references are from the New American Standard Bible, © 1960, 1962, 1963, 1968, 1971, 1972, 1973, 1975, and 1977 by The Lockman Foundation, and are used by permission.

Library of Congress Cataloging-in-Publication Data

Moore, June Hines
  You can raise a well-mannered child / June Hines Moore.
      p.   cm.
  Includes bibliographical references.
  ISBN 0-8054-6076-4 (pbk.)
  1. Child rearing.   2. Etiquette for children and teenagers.   3. Child rearing
—Religious aspects—Christianity.   I. Title.
HQ769.M597 1996
649'.1—dc20   96-13111
                                                                CIP

00 01 02 03 04   10 9 8 7 6

To my husband, Homer,
who gave me the freedom and
the continual encouragement
to write this book.
Being the gentleman he is,
he trained our sons,
Jeff and Greg,
who as young professionals
today are perfect gentlemen.
Well, no one is perfect.
My family calls me "Miss Grace"
when I make a gaffe
which is more often than one might expect.

Acknowledgments

God gave me the vision for the book and an understanding family, for which I am very grateful.

My family has graciously helped me free up the time to do research, to teach, and to write. My daughter-in-law, Leslie, has helped read the manuscript. She inspires me daily as I watch her and our son, Jeff, raise our granddaughters, Laura Elizabeth and Mary Catherine, to be well-mannered children. Our sons, Jeff and Greg, have steered me through many computer jungles, rescuing me from software nightmares. My husband, Homer, has "chauffeured" me to twenty-eight libraries, kept the books for Moore Than Manners Consulting, and assisted in my teaching.

My editor at Broadman & Holman Publishers, Janis Whipple, has been nice to work with and has taught me much about the publishing industry.

Contents

Introduction

Etiquette rules are of the head.

Manners are of the heart.

Together they are a shield against embarrassment.

That shield of etiquette rules and manners guards both ways. If we learn the rules and then adapt them to the manners in our heart, we will embarrass neither ourselves nor someone else.

For example, the president of a company called me to discuss a business etiquette workshop for his personnel. He said, "Mrs. Moore, we surely do need *eta-kwet* taught today." He obviously mispronounced our good English word *eta-kut* which we borrowed from the French, retaining the French pronunciation. The teacher in me wanted to correct him, for his own benefit of course, but my manners kept me silent. I would have embarrassed him.

There is a difference between etiquette and manners. Etiquette is a set of rules we memorize. Manners are more than that. They express how much we care about other people, their feelings, and their needs.

Good manners can create order out of the chaos in which we live. Manners are under our control because they flow from our heart. They give us the power to treat other people with kindness and respect, even when we don't feel like it.

The basis for good manners—consideration for others—never changes, but as we change millennia, we see our society change with new technology. Computers with the internet give us more information today than we accumulated in all the centuries past. We see our world shrink as travelers almost commute from continent to continent. We need civility as never before just to survive our ever-changing lifestyles. We need new rules and a few updated ones just to stay current—to keep us from embarrassing ourselves or someone else.

Home is where it all begins. While children are young, parents have the power to influence the way they behave. Parents have the opportunity to build character. It takes character to be polite when we would like to return rude for rude. Long ago, etiquette revealed one's good breeding. Today good manners portray a warm heart, good intentions, and self-respect regardless of one's economic status.

This book is my way of sharing with other parents what I have been blessed to learn through study and experience with many people in my classes. My students, young and old, come from all walks of life.

You will read in this book how good manners provide children with the tools to climb the ladder of success, but more important than business success is success that comes from living in harmony with God and other people. The Bible says in Luke 2:52 that "Jesus grew in wisdom and stature and in favor with God and man." That should be our goal as well.

I wrote this book, not to complicate your life, but to spark your imagination, to inspire you to study your child's temperament needs which may be different from yours, and finally to aid your efforts to build character, values, and polite behavior in your children.

PART I

. . .

Preparing "the Way"

Train up a child in the way he should go.

Proverbs 22:6

In a recent study at the Institute of Human Development at the University of California at Berkeley, psychologists found that a child's pro-social behavior is for the most part the result of his (or her) parents' training, and that the most powerful teachers for good and evil are indeed the mother and father.

God shows tremendous confidence in us when He gives us our children whom He created in His image. He knows that what our children are to be, they are now becoming.

Because our job as parents is not to be the manners police—hiding and trapping any slight offenders—we should prepare "the way" by finding our children's felt needs and motivating them accordingly. Felt needs are the internal, emotional needs of our individual personality. When those needs are met we feel good about ourselves and our surroundings.

1

. . .

Where Have All the Manners Gone?

One of the troubles in the world today is that we allowed the Golden Rule to become a bit tarnished.

Martin Vanbee

Every time I turned my back I heard snickering and muffled gasps. What was going on with my young, well-groomed charges at this their first etiquette class? Were they telling jokes? Maybe they were just embarrassed. Girls and boys are shy with each other at this age. The boys were probably showing off. Could this be a sign of trouble ahead?

This class of fifth graders represented some of the finest families in the city. On a gray Saturday morning in November, they gathered in Little Rock at the historic Capitol Hotel with all its formality and elegance—the ideal place to learn the finer points of social grace.

Built in 1876 the elegant hotel is reminiscent of a grand antebellum plantation mansion. Entering through the portico, we take an enchanting stroll back to a more romantic and genteel time. The ionic columns support the overhanging mezzanine just beneath a magnificent stained glass skylight. The lobby floor shines with mosaic tiles and daintily patterned carpet leading to an ornate, winding stairway to the mezzanine. The center of the lobby offers a plush tapestried sofa inviting guests to rest or wait for a companion.

From the lobby I watched my first two students arrive. Chauffeured by one or both of their parents and escorted through the doorway by the hotel valets, the children approached me as I greeted each of them. The frills and lace and stylish hair of pretty little girls impressed me with promise. The handsome young men wore ties with suits or sport coats and slacks, but expensive clothes were not the issue. I wanted to teach them to behave properly when they dressed in what we once called "our Sunday best."

Curious bystanders might think the children just left the funeral of their pet turtle. Their somber faces stared as though they were about to enter the principal's office for a scolding—or worse. These quiet, stiff, and docile children promised to be a dream class with no conduct problems. So far, I was elated with my first impression of these children.

Then one by one the girls sauntered over to the circular sofa in the center of the lobby. I saw each girl plop while spreading her legs as if straddling a seesaw. Obviously wearing dresses was not their daily custom. I knew right away we would need to work on a little feminine charm. That would be easy enough. What were the boys doing? They huddled over to the side. Some had their hands stuffed in their pockets, some jerked nervously at their ties, and still others tossed imaginary balls through the air. My first impression took on some tarnished edges, but after all, they were here to learn and I was in charge.

An hour later, however, my puzzlement at the snickering and hushed gasps now bordered on alarm. Suddenly, I whirled around and caught a glimpse of a roll sailing through the air and little Mary poking at her nose with a limp carrot sliver. Brian was dunking his white, starched napkin in his green broccoli soup, while Patty ate sugar cubes between courses.

You may have been born a princess,
but you will have to learn to be a lady.

A QUEEN OF ENGLAND
TO ONE OF HER GRANDDAUGHTERS

What had I gotten myself into? It's no wonder these caring, perceptive parents were so anxious to get their children in this class of limited enrollment. They must have thought I was a manners magician. I felt more like the manners police.

Was this class unusual? I don't think so. For me, it was only the first of many, each with its own set of antics and funny stories. Perhaps you, too, see uncivilized children everywhere. Have you ever dined with your child or grandchild in the school cafeteria? What about a fast-food place? Perhaps you see children today smacking gum, saying yeah, huh, and yep when they answer the telephone and yelling, "Hey Mom, it's for you!"

What is a parent to do? In an age when we go for hamburgers or tacos at the drive-up window, families no longer sit down together to eat a warm, quiet dinner where everyone discusses the events of the day. You know the kind—where parents instill values and philosophies into their children and lay firm, spiritual foundations. Family relationships grow deeper. Marriages grow stronger as partners teach their children how commitment looks and feels.

All is not lost. Just as computers and new technologies change our lifestyle, we have to look for creative ways to bring back old-fashioned manners and respect. I can't provide the needed twenty-six-hour day, but I can offer methods and fun activities that families can use to cultivate and nurture civility in our children—our leaders of tomorrow.

To be well mannered, our children must confidently meet and greet people, introduce themselves and others, use the telephone properly, become gracious hosts and guests, write thank-you notes, and dine gracefully.

Our moral and public behavior distinguishes us from animals. Parents today have an awesome responsibility, and we get little or no help from society. Something happened over the last twenty-five years that drastically changed our behavior. Kindness and consideration for others' feelings have traded places with "who cares?" and "what's in it for me?"

Times Have Changed

Where have all the manners gone? Perhaps they disappeared along with family values. One thing we do know: Rules of common courtesy are hardly ever taught in our public schools today, even though many teachers would, if they could. Also, children do not inherit good manners. They get them by growing up with parents who model and teach them. We might say that home is the classroom where students study their parents. How did we plummet from "Please" and "Thank-you" to "Yuk" and "Gimme"?

Parents are not necessarily at fault. Since the fifties our society has forced the proverbial pendulum to swing to the extreme. In less than a decade we went from the silver spoon mentality prevalent in the early part of this century to the hippies and free love of the sixties and seventies. That generation questioned the values and mores of the establishment. In most circles since then the prevailing attitude has been "Do your own thing," "If it feels good, do it," and "I'm not responsible." We find ourselves struggling to return to a more considerate and responsible society.

By the nineties we grew tired of the rudeness and crudeness. Actually, the corporate world noticed that young professionals were so socially inept they threatened the balance sheet. Business was lost because their highly skilled and well-educated young men and women chewed gum, neglected to introduce people, and stuffed their mouths with food while they tried to make the big sale over lunch with a client.

Corporations began seeking etiquette trainers and consultants to come in to smooth out the rough edges. Because money often motivates us where nothing else will, desperate executives are forcing the pendulum to swing the other way. We call it customer service. Of course, manners were originally God's idea. He gave us the Golden Rule which says we should treat others as we like to be treated. Today business publications of all kinds refer to the same rule we see in Matthew 7:12 and Luke 6:31.

Television still makes its contribution to the demise of socially acceptable behavior with popular comedy shows where the only polite person is a geek. The family with strong moral values is almost nonexistent on many programs. Even commercials for family shows advertise bad manners. Much of the rude behavior that we see in our children surfaces simply because they do not know the proper thing to do. It is that simple and that sad.

Our children deserve the opportunity to learn. We teach out of love and obedience to God's Word that tells us to nurture our children and build godly character in them. Showing consideration for others is part of that. Luke says that "Jesus grew...in favor with God and men" (Luke 2:52, NIV). The Bible doesn't give us Mary and Joseph's parenting plan, but it does say that with every charge or promise God shows us the way.

Pointing Our Children in the Right Direction

Why it is so important that we direct our children in the way they should go? Why can't we just let them make their own choices, which usually do not include showing consideration for anyone's needs but their own? Perhaps the answer lies in knowing that everything from plants to people grow in the direction we plant them.

Plants and children have a lot in common. Both grow in the direction that best meets their needs. When we turn a child toward God, he grows spiritually. When we turn him toward the way of the world, we take a quantum leap chance.

A plant grows toward the sun because its sustenance and growth must come from it. Our children will grow in the wrong direction, away from God, unless we teach them early that God alone will sustain them and meet their needs.

They need a strong early start, not just attending church to find the Lord, but seeing Him every day at home and in the lives of their parents who model good manners and reveal a personal relationship with the Lord. Spiritually, our children grow in the direction we point them. Will they grow straight or crooked?

When I was a child a very crooked tree grew in our backyard. It reached toward a neighbor's house so far the branches almost touched the ground. Why didn't that tree stand tall like the others nearby that reached skyward?

Years before, a tiny sprig of a sycamore tree emerged from the soil almost beneath the side wall of a building later removed. From its beginning, the small tree leaned toward the neighbor's house to escape the weight of the building while looking hungrily for the sunlight to give it life. That tree never reached skyward like the others, nor did it ever grow strong and tall. The sad-looking tree merely survived.

Like a tree, influences and forces mold a child from within. Someone compared a child to a piece of clay that we mold with our hands. But clay does not grow; clay is molded entirely from without. A child grows and matures from within and is more like a living plant that bears fruit, sometimes sweet and sometimes sour.

Biblical Examples of Parental Guidance

Social skills learned at home and at church produce the fruits of the Spirit listed in Galatians 5: love, joy, peace, patience, kindness, goodness, faithfulness, gentleness, and self-control. Teaching a child confidence in interpersonal skills can open doors to making friends, witnessing, and sharing God's Word.

Jesus' Early Leanings

Scripture affirms that *"Jesus grew in wisdom and stature and in favor with God and men"* (Luke 2:52, NIV). His parents pointed Him in the right direction from His youth. They took Him to the temple and no doubt taught Him at home.

According to *The Wycliffe Bible Commentary,* Jesus was not a child prodigy in the sense that He was abnormal. He had to mature and learn just as every child does today.[1] He even had to learn manners; yet He was perfect in every stage as He reached it.

Another biblical portrait of a child *"growing ... in favor both with the LORD and with men"* is young Samuel (1 Sam. 2:26).

His mother, Hannah, dedicated him to God before he was born. After Hannah nurtured and taught him, she kept her vow and took him to live at the temple. We know that Samuel became a great judge of the nation Israel.

Just as God chose Hannah, He chooses us to raise a specific child, whether we raise him or her in a two-parent home, a single-parent home, or in a grandparent's home. John 15:16 says "You did not choose Me, but I chose you, and appointed you, that you should go and bear fruit, and that your fruit should remain." If God gives us children, He gives us our most important and challenging fruit crop. We call it parenting.

However, just as no two families are identical, no two children are alike; therefore, we look for different ways of interacting to be effective. Children have "felt" needs for parents to discover. We see those needs by watching for signs and observing their responses and reactions to see what makes them feel good about themselves and their accomplishments.

Our Children's Needs

In the Seibert family Jeremy is reserved and introspective. John craves attention. No one would call him a loner. Just as these two guys react differently to people, they have different "felt" needs because they have different personalities. Jeremy's need may include striving for perfection. John may be interested in learning manners only if he can do it while having fun with his friends. He needs social interaction. An old adage says we can change the set of the sail but not the wind. We can change methods with Jeremy and John, but we should not try to change their natural bent.

Let's look at the felt needs of little Mary, Brian, and Patty in my first class at the Capitol Hotel. Mary and Brian were both outgoing, fun-loving children who liked the attention of their classmates any way they could get it. They were not hungry for attention at home. They needed peer approval and adult recognition because that was part of their personality makeup. The reason they stopped their antics almost in midair when I turned around was to gain the teacher's favor which also mattered to them.

Patty was quiet and observant. She wanted to please. It probably never occurred to her that one should not eat sugar cubes. She would never knowingly do anything to earn the disfavor of the teacher. Perhaps she came from a family that had banned all sweet treats from their home, and she had an insatiable sweet tooth.

We must use different approaches with Mary, Brian, and Patty to attract them to the manners table and keep them there without a battle. Battles rarely improve our manners.

Bad Manners or Bad Behavior

As much as we would like, we can't make children mannerly. We can help them want to be, but the "want to be" hinges on our satisfying their felt needs. I am not saying that if Johnny feels like acting out his tyrannical behavior, his parents should satisfy his felt need. Discipline with applied consequences should be used when the child has no choice in the matter. Safety and disrespect are examples. Polite behavior must emanate from the heart. We can make a child do the mannerly thing, and sometimes we should, but we cannot make them feel it. Our children are not puppets to be pulled in different directions and manipulated.

How difficult is it then to teach manners that come from the heart? Well, it doesn't take a college degree, a trade school diploma, a six-figure salary, expensive clothes, heirloom crystal, or a charm school certificate. It takes being aware of our child's felt needs, individual personalities, and reactions, and finally weaving techniques into our daily lives. After all, as Mark Twain said, cabbage is just cauliflower with a college education.

Conclusion

Yes, you *can* raise a well-mannered child without losing your own p's and q's, or your child. Learning manners can and should be fun. Children often think their parents spend hours dreaming up a bunch of silly rules just to lecture them and make their young lives miserable. Once they learn there is a reason for every rule of etiquette and that their lives can be more fun and comfortable, they are eager—well, maybe not eager, but more willing—to practice good social skills.

Psalm 139:13–18 describes how each child, unique in God's creation, is *"fearfully and wonderfully" made.* When we discover a child's natural bent, we usually find that child's felt need. Then we are on our way to raising children who are in favor with God and man.

2

. . .

Discovering Your Child's Personality

Just as the twig is bent, the tree's inclin'd.

Alexander Pope

The Vogul family has four children with no two alike. One child is shy and quiet, a real peacemaker. Another one is messy, but warm and friendly. The third child is a "neatnik," a veritable perfectionist. Then there is the one who thinks he knows everything and dominates his siblings with that power. How can four children in one family be so different? Each child has a natural, unique *bent*. It is noticeable almost from birth.

We do ourselves and our children a favor when we discover and nurture each child's unique temperament. Children's needs come from an inward motivation to meet their own natural drives, not ours. Children who fulfill a parent's need and not their own often grow up to be rebellious, withdrawn, irresponsible, or unable to cope in life.

Parents who nurture their child's natural bent are not permissive, indulgent pawns, catering to a child's every whim. God-given strength is necessary to bring out the temperament strengths in each child, to raise him or her to be in favor with God and man.

Using the following four temperament styles, you can identify which style best describes your own personality and discover the natural bent of each of your children. You can then nurture and guide them into the knowledge and practice of good manners.

Studying the temperament styles tempts all of us to label people or to put them in a box, so to speak. But labeling is bad manners, and it is not helpful. Naming the temperaments is simply a tool to help us understand others and ourself.

Identifying the Four P's of Personality

Four styles that begin with the letter *P* describe the unique temperaments of children and parents: *Powerful, Phun-Lover, Pleaser,* and *Perfecter.* Children have needs, not just for food, shelter, and clothing, but primary needs that suit their temperament. Whether that predominate need is leadership, fun, security, or time and answers, our children have a God-given inclination toward a certain bent. We call it their personality.

Personality Needs:
- *Choices (Powerful)*
- *Social Time (Phun-lover)*
- *Team Effort (Pleaser)*
- *Time and Answers (Perfecter)*

What Make Us Different?

Why so much difference in these children? To understand, we must look closer at the four temperament styles that have been around since the time of the Greeks. Today, we see a resurgent interest in discovering what makes each of us different in order to make the best of those differences.

Hundreds of years ago the Greeks named the four temperaments after these body fluids: Choleric, Sanguine, Phlegmatic, and Melancholy. Today we need updated and certainly more palatable terms such as The Powerful, The Phun-Lover, The Pleaser, and The Perfecter.

> *"The fountain of content must spring up in the mind,*
> *and he who hath so little knowledge*
> *of human nature as to seek happiness*
> *by changing anything but his own disposition,*
> *will waste his life in fruitless efforts*
> *and multiply the grief he proposes to remove."*
>
> SAMUEL JOHNSON

Each of us is a blend (see the chart on page 23), with one of four styles usually dominating our behavior, actions, and feelings. While maturing, children will behave in various ways at different stages of growth and development, but they will always resemble their inborn temperament. Child experts tell us that by age two a child will fit into a category displaying a unique blend of two styles. Other words for temperament and personality are *individualism, disposition, tendency, leaning,* and *makeup.*

Temperament and intelligence are not the same. Our temperament relates only to our personality. One style is not better than another. God made each of us unique for a reason. Imagine how boring life would be if we were all alike.

To raise a well-mannered child using information gleaned from the child's temperament we must draw a game plan, rather than a battle plan. As Dr. T. Berry Brazelton, the noted child psychologist, says, we must "Let him know that [we] respect his temperament."[1]

Some parents may be thinking: *That may work for a time, but what about next time, or when I am too busy or too tired to play the clean-up game? Not all chores can be fun, and when my children are adults they will share more than toys, whether they feel like it or not. It's my job to force some manners on them whether they like it or not.*

Sometimes children must do whatever the parent says with no questions asked; otherwise, we become manipulative or too permissive. If a parent considers the child's motivational need, the chore may get done or the lesson in manners learned with fewer hassles and less grief.

Motivational needs are:
- *Opportunity to lead (Powerful)*
- *Social approval (Phun-lover)*
- *Peace and harmony (Pleaser)*
- *Time to do quality work (Perfecter)*

Children seldom tell us what they need. They may not even know, but they act out their self-interest needs. Are all needs good? Those needs that enhance a child's sense of godly self-worth are the best. Children who see themselves as loved by their parents and by God are the ones most likely to use the good manners of kindness and consideration for others. We build self-worth, confidence, and generosity in our children when we take time to consider each child's natural bent.

One pattern will usually describe a child when he or she is not with family members, but one pattern cannot define a child. The birth order of a child, parenting styles, and sibling relationships all play a part in a child's behavior at home. Usually, the true pattern emerges when the child is with strangers.

A Test to Determine the Pattern

Imagine that you are holding your baby, and an old friend that you have not seen in years comes to visit. After the two of you talk, the longtime friend admires your handsome child and holds outstretched arms to embrace him.

The outgoing, Phun-Loving child is eager to make a new friend and have some fun. He smiles a big, toothless grin and leans toward the stranger. The outgoing, Powerful child may allow the unfamiliar person to take him, but show little emotion.

The reserved child who is a Pleaser, likes to make others happy, but he does not like meeting unfamiliar people or situations. He may turn away, or he may reluctantly let the stranger take him. This child seldom makes a fuss. The reserved child, who is the cautious Perfecter, may glare at the stranger and even resist any overtures toward him.

After the test or experiment of seeing how our child responds to an unfamiliar face, we must be careful not to put him or her in a box—none of our children fit into a one-pattern mold. Each child is different. You may be thinking: *My child has characteristics in all the categories.* Most children do, but if we select one or two groups best suited to our child, we find some insights into how to teach each child. After all, we want our children to be mannerly, have friends, get a job and keep it.

The Importance and Uniqueness of Each Temperament

No single pattern or blend is preferable over another. Each temperament has strengths and weaknesses, but God made each of us, imperfections and all, for a special purpose and mission in life. As parents we must appeal to our child's strengths without ignoring his or her weaknesses, remembering that a strength carried to extreme becomes a weakness.

Some examples: When Powerfuls carry the strength of leadership to an extreme, they become intolerant, like a tyrant in control. When Phun-Lovers carry the strengths of friendliness and enthusiasm to an extreme, they become overindulgent and overbearing. When Pleasers carry the strength of cooperativeness to an extreme, they become compromising and lacking in initiative. When Perfecters carry the strength of correctness to an extreme, they become impatient and rigid. If you have a true Perfecter, encourage him or her to strive for the best but to remember that only God can achieve perfection—"He who began good work in you will perfect it until the day of Christ Jesus" (Phil. 1:6).

The Powerfuls and the Phun-Lovers are usually more visible and get more recognition, but the Pleasers and the Perfecters are in the background, supporting and holding up the standards to fulfill 2 Timothy 2:15: "Be diligent to present yourself approved to God as a workman who does not need to be ashamed, handling accurately the word of truth." If any one of us fulfills God's purpose for our lives, we are truly successful.

Parenting with Style

We need to know our own style so we can be more effective with our children's natural bent.

- The Powerful is a take-charge, no-nonsense parent.
- The Phun-Lover parent is often permissive, but oh what fun that mom and dad can be. This parent is like one of the kids, and that delights the children.
- The Pleaser parent might answer yes to these questions: "Am I easygoing? Am I a good listener with a fair amount of patience?"
- The Perfecter parent is cautious, conscientious, composed, logical, and self-sacrificing.
- Both the Powerful and the Perfecter can be domineering —expecting and demanding much from a child.

Quizzing Mom and Dad for Style

The following scenario provides another glimpse into the parenting styles. Mom prepares delicious, strawberry tarts for

Megan and her friends after Saturday's ball practice. When the girls hit the door and sniff the aroma they are famished. Mom talks to the girls while Megan brings in the tray to serve her guests. Tripping over the rug, Megan takes a spill and so do the plates, dropping the yummy strawberries on Mom's spotless floor.

Without knowledge of the four temperament styles, Mom might respond in one of these ways:

1. The Powerful parent wants control with little thought for others' feelings: "Now, look what you have done! What made you do such a thing? You are so clumsy." Notice the "what" question and the accusations.

2. The Phun-Lover parent makes everything a game. Having fun is more important than the homemade tarts. The Phun-Lover parent might say, "Uh, oh, oops. Let's all pitch in and see how fast we can clean this up." Who can get the mop first? Notice the "who" questions. These parents want fun and approval.

3. The Pleaser parent wants a minimum of conflict. That parent might say, "Oh, that is all right, honey. How can I help? Oh, I know. I will get the mop while you pick up the dishes. We can find another treat to serve." Feelings and teamwork concern this parent. Notice the "how" question.

4. The Perfecter parent, a stickler for rules, wants perfection. This mom says, "Why did you get in such a hurry? If you had done it the way I taught you, you would not have made the mess and spoiled our desserts." Notice the "why" question, the criticism, and the way to prevent something—Do it the way I taught you.

Playing the Baseball Game

See how you think each parent would respond in this scenario. A young lad strikes out for the second time in one baseball game.

- The Powerful parent who is competitive and results-oriented might say,
  "_____."

- The Phun-Lover parent who is concerned about social approval might say,
  "_____."

- The Pleaser parent usually has little ambition. This mom or dad may bring the boy to the game late and say,
  "_____."

- The Perfecter parent might say,
  "_____."

The correct way to respond should be based on the child's natural bent—the child's personality need, not the parent's. A parent who thinks only of his or her needs might respond like this:

- The Powerful Parent—"I always win. _Why_ can't you? What made you hesitate?"
- The Phun-Lover Parent—"You made me look bad. Think about _who_ you are?"
- The Pleaser Parent—"Who cares? _How_ much does it matter, anyway?"
- The Perfecter Parent—"I told you I know best. You should have practiced more when I told you to work on it. _Why_ didn't you?"

Notice _what, who, how, why._

The next exercise will help parents identify a temperament style and respond appropriately to the child's need. In chapter 1 we talked about changing the set of the sail, not the wind. When we change our methods to suit our child's temperament need, we change the set of the sail. Only God can change the wind. Following are some proper responses.

- To the Powerful Child: "I noticed that you really played hard. *What* do you think we could do to improve your batting average for the next game?" (This child fears losing control of his situation.)
- To the Phun-Lover Child: "You inspire me with your enthusiasm even when you hit a fly ball. Let's think of someone *who* could give us some batting tips." (This child fears loss of social approval. He or she likes involvement with others.)
- To the Pleaser Child: "You stick with the task even if you don't succeed the first time. You take the time to get things right. *How* can I help you improve for the next game?" (This child fears change from the status quo and loss of stability.)
- To the Perfecter Child: "You always do your best and try to improve your game. Tomorrow you'll get another chance. This one game won't make the season. *Why* don't we practice when we get home? I'll pitch for you. (This child fears not meeting a self-imposed standard of perfection.)

Examining the Four P's Biblically

Just as we parent our children, God parents us, always considering our natural bent. In His Word He gives us glimpses of the behavior styles of His children and how He matured them, bringing out their strengths and overcoming their weaknesses.

After his conversion, Paul became a great missionary and champion for the Lord. As a blend of Powerful and Perfecter, he admitted to never achieving perfection (see Rom. 7:15 and 19). Simon Peter was a Phun-Lover. Before he followed the Lord's teaching, his bent was to be a talkative, know-it-all fisherman, often seen with "his foot in his mouth." John 18:10 says that Peter rashly cut off the ear of the slave of the high priest. Earlier when the Lord told them He would be crucified, Peter emphatically said no, that he would not let such a thing happen. We see in Matthew 26:69–75 that Peter was impulsively wrong again. Yet in Acts 2 Peter became a great preacher at Pentecost where three thousand people were saved. Impulsive Peter became the courageous disciple ready to go to prison and even death.

If Christ had that much trouble with His "children," maybe our children's behavior shouldn't surprise us. Without doubt, parenting is difficult. *"Bringing our children up in the discipline and instruction of the Lord" is not easy* (Eph. 6:4), but maturing our children to be *"in favor with God and men"* can be done if we have the right information and motivation.

Conclusion

Each parent and each child is a blend of the four basic patterns. One temperament dominates. When we know our individual style and that of our child, we usually know his or her felt need. Then we have options to motivate and encourage each child to use good manners based on a felt need that emanates from the child's natural, God-given bent.

Proverbs 22:6 tells us to "train up a child in the way he [or she] should go." "Literally, according to his way, or the child's habits and interests. The instruction must take into account his [or her] individuality and inclinations, and be in keeping with his degree of physical and mental development."[2]

Because each child is a blend of temperaments with one predominating, this book cannot explain how to teach each skill according to every temperament combination. That much information would fill a set of encyclopedias.

As parents we know our children best. We know that our adult need is not always the same as our child's. Keeping our child's natural bent in mind, we adapt skills and methods to suit our family.

Many methods and techniques in this book lend themselves to all temperaments. My hope is that parents will teach manners in a way that all the family will enjoy. That includes teaching proper behavior when the children don't even realize it. Parents teach when they model, provide learning opportunities, make positive comments, and teach little by little. A well-mannered child is not "mannered" in a day; it takes time.

Parents are teachers, not the manners police. With a little planning, we can raise our children to show kindness and consideration for others, guiding them to be *in favor with God and men.*

PERSONALITIES IN THE BIBLE (Ken Voges, Biblical Personal Profiles)	
Powerful	*Paul* (Gal. 2); *Lydia* (Acts 16:13–15); *Sarah* (Gen. 16)
Phun-Lover	*Peter* (Matt. 16; 26; Acts 3); *Miriam* (Exod. 2; 15:20–21); *Rebekah* (Gen. 24)
Pleaser	*Barnabas* (Acts 4:36–37; 9:26–27; 12–13); *Abraham* (Gen. 21–24); *Hannah* (1 Sam. 1–2); *Martha* (Luke 10:38–42)
Perfecter	*Moses* (Exod. 3–4; 20; 32); *John* (John 19:26–27); *Esther* (Esther 4); *Ruth* (Ruth 2:2, 10; 3:1–18)

Each Child Is a Blend of Four Temperaments with one predominant

THE POWERFUL CHILD

- Outgoing
- Goal/task-oriented
- Bossy and controlling
- Needs challenges, choices, results
- Likes action

- Asks "what" questions

- Motivated to control his world
- Fears loss of control

THE PHUN-LOVING CHILD

- Outgoing
- Fun-loving
- A real people person
- Relationships more important than tasks
- Responds better to praise than any other
- Asks "who" questions
- Needs social time
- Motivated to talk and seek approval
- Fears loss of social approval

THE PLEASER CHILD

- Reserved
- A people pleaser
- Follower
- Peacemaker
- Team player
- Easygoing
- Iron will

- Asks "how" questions
- Needs patience, harmony

- Motivated to cooperate
- Fears conflict and loss of stability
- Likes routine

THE PERFECTER CHILD

- Reserved
- Particular
- Low energy level
- Likes lists of accomplishments
- Strives for perfection
- Likes to know reason for everything
- Asks "why" questions
- Needs time to do quality work
- Motivated to follow the rules
- Fears failure of performance

3

. . .

Parents and the Manners Police

Home is where children learn 95 percent

of the things they take with them into life.

Thomas Armstrong, *Awakening Your Child's Genius*

We can lead a child to the dinner table, even bribe him to eat his broccoli, but we cannot make him like it. So it is with making children mannerly. We can make them smile and say polite words, making us look like strong parents, but in reality good manners must spring from a heartfelt response of kindness and consideration. The dour-faced manners police can't illicit those feelings. Perhaps that is the reason the Scripture puts "in favor with God" before the part "and with men" (Luke 2:52, NIV). God is in the heart-changing business.

God designed parents to be the built-in teachers of their children. Teaching is part of our job description because we are our children's first teacher; therefore, our normal daily activities can be great stimuli to develop a child's confidence in relating to others. Because children are often immune to anyone's feelings except their own, we must guide them. Daily opportunities arise for us to model, instruct, demonstrate, encourage, praise, and develop a planned, positive approach based on their self-interest needs. The goal is to inspire feelings and actions that show sensitivity to others.

Dr. Gary Peterson, a clinical associate professor of psychiatry at the University of North Carolina at Chapel Hill, says today's children are at a real disadvantage if parents do not teach them to be sensitive to the feelings of others. He says if we do not teach children manners, "we are robbing them of some of their vocabulary of behavior."[1]

Teaching without Preaching

The key to stimulating the desire to be mannerly is seeing Mom or Dad enjoy being courteous, whether it's teaching a rule of proper decorum or opening a door. Encouraging our child to learn anything whether it's a fact, a skill, a chore, or a principle becomes easier when we show excitement and provide opportunities. Our confidence in our child's ability to learn inspires him or her to practice the rules when we least expect. Teaching our children costs us only a little time and energy, but our efforts reap great benefits.

We can weave this teaching into our family's everyday life. Some examples of this are:

- With genuine excitement we make comments to our children such as: "I learned something new today," or "A friend told me about a book that will show me how to . . . ," or "I read an interesting article today," or "I have been wondering about . . . Why don't we look it up?"
- We laughingly tell stories of how we have been embarrassed over certain mistakes or gaffes because we did not know better.

- We provide opportunities for learning when we take a child to a museum, an art gallery, an exhibition, the library, a play or invite friends over on the weekend or after an athletic event or after church. It may be obvious, but children must interact with people to learn people skills. We also must actively involve them in our teaching process.

We learn best by doing. Someone summed it up this way:

Tell me, and I will forget.
Show me, and I may understand.
Involve me, and I will experience it.
Then it is mine forever.

In learning anything new, some children need to be in on the decision making and feel some degree of control. Some children need activity and people cheering for them. Other children want to try the activity with a parent or a friend, perhaps in a team. Others prefer to learn the rules—anything that will help them do it right. They want to learn to satisfy their sense of accomplishment. The first child wants control, and the second one wants fun and social approval. The third one is a team player, and the fourth child wants to do everything just right.

After you have identified the personality blend of your child, look for signs of what makes your child feel good about himself or herself and his or her accomplishments. Ask the question often: What would make my child want to know more?

Whetting the Appetite

We must interest our child in learning before we begin. Some lessons are more interesting to young children than others. Learning formal dining is not one of their favorites, but when puberty sets in, they think of dating, graduation dinners, and job interviews. We all need incentives. In filling the need we and our child have fun learning. Our child develops a particular people skill, and we are rewarded by seeing them grow in respect from others.

Ways to Teach Manners

As parents we should model positively, create an environment for learning manners, look for that internal motivation that will involve our children, and teach age-appropriate rules.

Modeling the Manners

Children learn from our example. The problem is they can't tell the difference between a good example and a bad one. Modeling good manners may be our easiest and most convenient method of teaching appropriate behavior. It's up to us to make sure we know the rules and show honor, dignity, and respect to others. Modeling shows and tells the behavior we want our children to imitate. Proper modeling engages our children in the learning process. How? Perhaps, unconsciously, our children learn by seeing us use a napkin, cut meat properly, and open doors for others. Children hear us say please and thank-you and I'm sorry. They see us wait for a turn to speak.

We wish that modeling good manners was enough, but we know that the opportunity to engage in every social skill does not arise everyday. Most of us do not use bone china, lead crystal, and lace tablecloths unless it is a special occasion. We don't often dress in formal attire. But when those times arise (and they will), we feel better about ourselves when we know the rules and how to conduct ourselves.

Develop a Positive Attitude

Developing a positive attitude is another method that works with all children. Sometimes tired, frustrated parents harp over the main course, over dessert—even over the cleaning up. It is little wonder that our children turn a deaf ear to "Don't do that." "Don't act that way." "Don't, don't, don't."

Out of time and out of patience we tend to accentuate the negative only to learn that a negative attitude is contagious. A negative word is like a drop of ink in a pitcher of water. It takes thirteen pitchers of clean water to bring back the clarity.

We can't expect our children to get excited about learning a long list of rules if we are dejected and sullen. With enthusiasm and planning, there is no limit to what we can teach. Enthusiasm is also contagious.

No matter the temperament, we must be positive with our children, saying, "Yes, that is the way," or "Now watch me do it again." If children don't get it right after a few tries, they are trying to tell us something. They are not ready for that skill because of maturity, dexterity, coordination, or for another reason. Proverbs 25:11 tells us "like apples of gold in settings of silver, is a word spoken in right circumstances."

Ideally, parents should present a united front as models of good behavior. If not, one parent must practice the rules of etiquette without commenting. Having good manners means not ever criticizing the other parent's social graces or lack of them. One or both parents should recognize any family member's attempt to be mannerly.

Motivating, not Manipulating

Sometimes we become so eager to see proper behavior that we try to manipulate our children. Manipulating is trying to get something from people they do not want to give. Parents who resort to manipulation may have the best intentions, but they often use crafty influences to control a child's behavior. "The boogey man will get you if you go in there," Dad warns, or "I am leaving now," Mom announces as she moves out of sight, hoping her child will follow because he's afraid of losing his mom. She manipulates him with fear.

Motivation outweighs any attempts at manipulation. To motivate is to find a latent desire and arouse it. The desire is there because, by nature, we all want to know "what's in it for me?"

The two kinds of motivation are external and internal. Internal motivation is more likely to result in positive action. For example, a savvy job seeker says, "I am going to wear a stiff shirt and creased trousers instead of my jogging suit to the interview because I want the job." Internal motivation results in positive action—practicing good manners to get a job.

What about external motivation? Visualize a family meal where both parents make positive comments to their seven-year-old. Dad says, "How nice, Daniel! You remembered to put the napkin in your lap. I know it is hard to remember that, but Mom and I enjoy our meal with you more when you wipe the spaghetti sauce off your mouth before drinking your milk."

Mom says, "I can understand what you say better when you finish chewing before telling me about John tripping over the teacher's foot at school today. That must have been a hoot!"

The Perfecter parents and the Powerful parents sometimes neglect the positive in favor of the negative. The Powerful parent has little patience, and the Perfecter parent is intent on teaching every nuance of each rule. Impatience and overzealousness leave little room for positive teaching.

Powerful and Perfecter parents may attempt to discipline good manners into their children. Bad manners are not necessarily commensurate with acts of disobedience. When a young child knocks over a glass of milk, it may be neither bad manners nor disobedience. It's more likely to be undeveloped coordination.

All four styles can produce parents who criticize, nag, or belittle. Children raised in that environment develop a defeatist attitude. They lack confidence in their ability to interact successfully with others. Stubbornly forcing a please before giving a treat to a toddler does not teach consideration which is the goal. Suggesting or reminding a child to say please is helpful. Demanding perfect behavior sows seeds of bitterness and rebellion (see Heb. 12:15).

The following story poignantly shows how a child's need may differ from the parent's need.

"When I do good, I do bad, and when I do bad, I do it real good," young Chase confessed to his mom.

"I do well," scolded his mom. "Do is a verb. You must modify it with an adverb."

No matter what grade young Chase was in, he didn't need a stinging critique. His mother heard his words but not the message he was trying to give her. His mother, of all the people in his life, should listen with her heart, not her English teacher ears.

The grammar lesson could have waited. Mom could have said something like, "Tell me, Chase, why you feel that way." Mom was focusing on her need. As a former teacher, I've had to bite my tongue more than once. Perhaps Chase's mom could have done that.

If we want showcase manners, we must examine our motivation. The purpose of this book is to help parents raise children who feel confident in their manners, not parrots and certainly not obsequious sycophants. I know those are strong words, but they go to the heart of what manners is all about—consideration for others. Children who feel arrogant and superior will have poor people skills because they displace the right focus; they think only of self.

If we know the rules, we will find it easier to think of others before self. Confidence makes us feel good about being nice to others, and then we are "in favor with God and men." What our children need from us is not forced, dictator-style manners training but fun, modeling, gentle reminders, praise, and time.

Teach Age-Appropriate Rules

Finally, when should we begin age-appropriate training?

Which rules should we zero in on, and which ones should we postpone for later? Elizabeth Post, noted etiquette expert, says to "start as soon as possible."[2] As cute and loveable as our babies are, they leak from every orifice and have no manners. They are not at all considerate, especially at 2:00 A.M. when they awaken sleep-deprived parents.

Should we begin teaching before birth? A grandmother told me her adult children have lost their senses. They talk and read to their unborn baby; yet child development experts say reading to a child in utero is good parenting.

Certainly by the time children reach school age, they need to know how to treat friends and acquaintances with respect. Their peers and superiors will judge their behavior. Children are some-times heartless and even unmerciful to their classmates. When children say please and thank-you, they can and do mimic their parents. That's a good time to begin.

Most three-year-olds are ready to learn to use a napkin, not talk with food in their mouths, and not sing at the table. By age five most children can hold a spoon properly—not like a sand shovel.

Letitia Baldrige in *Manners for the '90s* says "by age of ten" children should "be reasonably well-socialized human beings, aware of almost all of the important tenets of good manners, lacking only the adult polish."[3]

The following list is a guide to realistic goals for appropriate age groups.

Age three to four:
- Saying hello and good-bye
- Saying please and thank-you
- Shaking hands

Age four to five:
- Saying excuse me
- Using a fork and spoon properly
- Asking for food to be passed

- Using a napkin
- Talking without a mouth full of food

Age five to six:
- Proper behavior for a reasonable amount of time in public places, such as not making a scene or talking too loudly.

Age six to ten:
- Not interrupting others
- Saying excuse me when interrupting becomes necessary
- Showing respect for the disabled
- Offering help when it is needed
- Showing respect for elders, such as allowing older people to enter or exit first, speaking respectfully, and offering assistance.
- Refraining from making hurtful comments or judgments, such as "Your ears are too big" or "That's an ugly dress."
- Good manners when visiting
- Making the bed
- Writing thank-you notes

Age ten to twelve:
- Exercising discretion: Keeping family secrets is extremely difficult for children under twelve because children listen when they appear uninterested.
- Respond when spoken to
- Speak softly when calling someone to the telephone
- Refrain from sassing
- Respect property at home and away
- Answer the telephone properly
- Keep his or her room clean and picked up
- Do assigned chores cheerfully, punctually, and efficiently
- Play music at a reasonably low decibel
- Respect the privacy of others
- Wait one's proper turn in line
- Say excuse me when bumping into someone
- Attend to one's guest
- Write thank-you notes for gifts, overnight visits, and special treats of any kind
- Be punctual
- Respect the driver of the car

- Deposit trash in proper receptacle
- Observe rules of safety such as walking, biking,
  skating
- Be kind to animals
- Respect others' privacy, including siblings

Age twelve to twenty:
- Observing house rules about the noise level
  (especially music)
- Leaving sufficient gas in the tank of the family car
- Not blocking the driveway
- Cleaning up after parties
- Not receiving or making late-night phone calls
- Not having friends visit when parents are away

Panic! Seeing such a list of expectations brings on the lecturing, correcting, and admonishing, but the more we tell, the more our kids rebel. Both telling and showing manners to our children are important, but unless we involve them and fill a self-interest need, the effort to teach will likely be futile.

While it is true that if we aim at nothing we will surely hit our target, as parents we can relax and enjoy our children because life is a potpourri of trial and error, success and failure. Our children do not learn the finer points of proper decorum in one day.

We have a built-in way of understanding our children. We interact with them daily from their birth. God lends them to us for a few years with a charge to train and nurture them. By developing people skills, our children's future success is enhanced in all areas.

Manners and discipline are not the same. We don't have to be the manners police. With the right information we involve our children while looking for their needs, modeling before them with a positive approach, motivating them according to felt-needs, and choosing age-appropriate skills to teach how to be in favor with God and men.

PART II

• • •

Teaching People Skills

About 15% of one's financial and career success

is due to technical skills while the remaining 85%

is due to people skills

Sherwin Williams Company News

G ood manners were God's idea first. Long before mankind learned that courtesy and kindness made our lives more enjoyable, He gave us the Golden Rule: "Do to others what you would have them do to you" (Matt. 7:12, NIV). Someone has said that good manners were devised to act as a buffer between individuals in collision, and every meeting of individuals is a collision.

While it is important to know a sorbet spoon from a coffee spoon, perhaps more importantly, our children need to learn how to meet and talk to people, how to thank them properly, and how to be gracious hosts and oft-invited guests.

The chapters in this section will give you some fun and creative ways to teach those skills.

4

. . .

Mouth Manners
and Other Menaces

*I will guard my ways, that I may not sin with my
tongue; I will guard my mouth as with a muzzle.*

Psalm 39:1

Most of us are born using our mouths to get what we
want, especially from family members. Coping with
manners of the tongue is one of our biggest challenges
as parents. We begin with the basics such as saying please and
thank-you and excuse me and I'm sorry. Modeling is the best way
to teach these people skills. From the time a baby can smile, we
can say, "Thank you for being a happy baby." These people skills
can and should be habit forming. They work like learning magic
words. We instruct children to say them and then remind them
in a friendly tone of voice when the need arises. For instance,
"What's the magic word?"

It is important to remind a child *before* an infraction instead of
scolding him or her after the fact. Showing impatience and anger

over forgetfulness often creates a negative and harmful experience. Stubbornly depriving her of a cookie to punish her for forgetfulness causes disharmony, discord, and counter-productive results.

When Suzie is old enough, Mom and Dad should make sure she understands that saying please and thank-you just to get what she wants is not appropriate. Showing consideration for others, making others happy, will make her feel good.

Specific Mouth Manners

Greeting Properly

Erma Bombeck said, "A grunt is never acceptable. Hello is nice."

Greetings such as hello are also among the basics. Before going to visit the next-door neighbor, Mom can gently remind, not demand, that Hank say hello to Mrs. Smith. This works much better than scolding the child later or embarrassing him in front of Mrs. Smith. Children should always be taught to say hello to their parents' guests. When a child enters the room and sees an adult friend of Mom's, he or she should say, "Hello, Mrs. Peters," or a similar recognition. When Mrs. Peters says, "Hello, Melissa, How are you?" Melissa should respond. If Melissa does not answer, her mom can gently prod her with "Mrs. Peters asked how you are," but it is tiresome for children when a parent continually asks them to show off their good manners. We go to extremes when we repeatedly say, "Can't you smile for the nice Mrs. Hilltop?" or "Now give Aunt Matilda a big hug and kiss."

Saying Please, Thank-You, and Excuse Me

Another basic is saying please and thank-you. The surest way to get our children to say these nuggets of gold is to say them often ourselves and give gentle reminders, such as: "And what do you say?" after giving a treat to the child. "Please, say please" is the polite way of teaching. The child hears the word twice. Used honestly, these simple expressions grease the friction of human inter-action.

Saying I'm Sorry

A forced "I'm sorry" may not be worthwhile when it is spoken but not felt. Parents disagree on this topic. Some say a child should always be forced to express an apology, because saying I'm sorry often enough will eventually become a natural response. Others tell me it forces a child to lie.

I have talked to childcare experts, including one who has successfully worked with young children for more than twenty-five years. She encourages those in her care to say "I am sorry." If they will not, she says, "Chris, I wish you could say you are sorry." Then she makes the apology herself after the offender refuses. "I am sorry Chris broke your toy, Josh. Let me see if I can repair it." Teaching by example may be the best way to teach children to say I'm sorry. We can feel only our own regret, not another's. Let's look at the situation when it is our child who should apologize.

Scene: Clint pushes the boy. Mom says, "Say you're sorry,"

Clint responds, "Why should I? He cut in line ahead of me."

If Mom lashes out in anger with her tongue, she provokes the child to more anger. Ephesians 6:4 says "Do not provoke your children to anger." She might try talking to Clint covering these four points.

1. Anger is a natural emotion. We can harbor it, letting it eat away at us, or we can find appropriate ways to vent it, causing the anger to lose its ugly grip on us.
2. Lashing out can destroy relationships.
3. When we take the first step and apologize, we usually feel better, knowing we took the mature path of dealing with the unpleasantness.

4. Mom might remind Clint that it takes a big man (or woman) to say I'm sorry.

Hand in hand with apologies goes forgiveness, especially when we have been wronged. Mom might say, "The way I forgive others, Clint, when they hurt me is to remember all the times I need God to forgive me for my actions or reactions."

Making some children say they are sorry, when all persons involved know they are not, only makes the perpetrators resentful and defiant. Parents know their children best. Some children respond easily when encouraged to express compassion and regret. Others take a little longer—the Powerfuls and Perfecters usually. There is no statute of limitations on making an apology. Sometimes, the child will express regret later after thinking about it.

Not Responding with Yeah and Yo

In the South many parents continue to teach their children to say "Yes, ma'am" and "No, sir." Other parents choose to teach "Yes, Dad" and "No, Mom." Either way is better than "yeah" and "yo."

Accepting Compliments

When a compliment comes, accept it graciously and say thank-you. For some reason females tend to make excuses or express a putdown of whatever someone admires. Boys, on the other hand, often ignore complimentary comments. They should both say, "Thank-you."

Scene: Ramona says, "Oh, I like your new shoes," to which Sarah replies, "Oh, these old things. I got them days ago." Or Sarah stares silently and blankly at the shoes as though she didn't know they were down there.

With proper training Sarah can smile and say, "Thank-you," or "You are nice to say so," or "Thank-you for noticing." The response should suit Sarah's personality.

If Sarah just stares at Ramona or crosses her feet and looks at the floor, her mom may reply, "Oh, how nice of you to notice." After a few such incidents, Sarah will pick up the phrasing and confidently say it for herself.

Specific Mouth Manners

Other menaces of the mouth that destroy harmony in the home include lying, quarrelling, contradicting, interrupting, and making loud outbursts. All temperaments erupt into these with the right provocation, especially in the safe harbor of home.

Telling the Truth with Tact

The truth sometimes hurts, and children can be brutally honest. Teaching a young child to be honest and yet not offend is a challenge. Young children do not easily understand the difference between truth and fiction, nor do they understand how words wound others.

Your daughter sees an older lady with a color rinse on her otherwise gray hair and blurts out, "Look, Mom, that woman has blue hair."

Quietly and gently draw your child's attention to some aspect about herself that might cause her feelings to be hurt if someone shouted, "Your new hair cut makes you look like a boy!" Or remind her of a time when someone hurt her feelings. Do not shame. Do not blame, just calmly explain.

Scene: It is your daughter's sixth birthday. "Why should I say thank-you when I don't like the gift, Mom? You told me to always tell the truth!" Suzie exclaims.

Explain to Suzie that she can thank Aunt Mary for giving her the tea set when she really wanted a bat and ball. Thanking someone for a kindness is not a lie. Teach her to thank the person for thinking about her. Mom will find that a better time to cover this subject is *before* the party.

Dealing with Lying

Some lies are more serious and reap greater consequences, but lying is lying and little ones set the pattern. Parents who model with so-called white lying often find to their amazement that their children lie without compunction.

Scene: The telephone rings. "Tell Mr. Abernathy that I am not at home." Later that dad hears his son tell a sibling to lie for him.

In talking with your children, tell stories of how lies have hurt people you know. Show them how one lie calls for another. Lying about someone may rob him or her of a good reputation.

Reading stories about telling the truth especially appeals to Pleasers and Perfecters. William Bennett's *Book of Virtues, Aesop's Fables,* and Bill Gothard's *Character Sketches* are among the many good books. Explain what bearing false witness means in the Bible. It is the ninth commandment God gave us in Exodus 20:16: You shall not bear false witness against your neighbor.

Talk about the reward of feeling good when we do the right thing. Logical consequences or some other appropriate discipline may be necessary if a child has been instructed properly and still chooses to disobey.

For serious lying problems that could produce a pathological liar, seek professional help early.

Settling Sibling Quarrels

One method for calming sibling quarrels is collecting marbles in a jar. School teachers use such a jar to keep score and reward good behavior among their students. Starting with an empty jar, add marbles for good manners and remove them for bad ones. At the end of the week reward them with a special treat that you and the children planned. Make sure the children are old enough to understand how the system works. The technique works best if both children are held responsible for the behavior of the two of them. That way each child will want to help the other one stay out of trouble—more marbles in the jar mean more rewards.

If you have no marbles, or your children are young enough to swallow them, put nickels or quarters in a jar placed on top of the refrigerator and buy a surprise treat at the end of the week or month with the money that survived the quarrels test.

Use games, badges, bulletin boards, refrigerator displays, or puppets to stimulate harmony in the family. The Powerful likes challenges. The Phun-Lover likes games. The Pleaser likes team work, and the Perfecter likes time and specific instructions on how to make a perfect score. One mother made a Care-Bear type character to be worn as a badge of honor for her son and an angel traced around a cookie cutter for her daughter when they showed good manners.

Quarrels at the dinner table were fewer after Mary Ann calmly had her children carry their dinner trays to their respective rooms to eat alone and without television viewing. This bold mom left the dirty dishes in there for them to smell and look at for a week. Week-old tuna fish casserole cured the constant grumbling at meal time. Of course, it is not every mom that could endure that herself.

Being in favor with men in general is often easier than keeping siblings in favor with one another. Once the squabbling begins, what can a parent do? Should the parent intervene?

With our two strong-willed children, I found that manners of the tongue were the most difficult to deal with. When I used my tongue to try to stop their conflicts, they got worse, and I ended up in the middle.

Finally, I learned to ignore most of their quarrels unless they became abusive verbally or physically. Children often try to get our attention any way they can, even if it brings reprimand.

The following scene is an example of a typical argument in

many households at the dinner table and one dad's solution: Change the subject, divert the attention of the quarrelers.

Scene: "It's my turn to have a friend sleep over this weekend," Robert barks at the dinner table.

"No, it is my turn," growls his sister, Belinda.

Dad: "That subject can wait until after dinner. How was practice today, Robert? Belinda?" He diverted the subject to a personal interest of each child.

Nancy, a mother of three boys, used humor to settle squabbles. She had her boys embrace when they got into a fight. They usually began laughing instead of fighting. That may not work with everybody, but it is worth a try.

Interrupting

Without warning, children take their chances and jump into conversations as the mood strikes them. They may recognize only their need to be heard at any cost. The word *interrupting* is not in their vocabulary; or if it is they ignore the rules about it.

We must explain that interrupting is talking while another person is speaking. Someone aptly said it was like knocking someone off the sidewalk.

If we give children their fair chance to speak, they eventually learn the rules. The following are some ways to teach conversational skills.

1. When we finish a sentence or our story, we tell the child that it is now his or her turn to speak. We must remember to keep our story brief; children are short on attention ability.

2. Conversation is like playing ball. One person pitches and another catches. A parent makes a comment, pitching a ball to the child and instructing him to make his comment after he catches the ball.

3. For an extreme remedy, we can interrupt the child every time he opens his mouth to show him how it feels. Use this technique only as a game when the subject matter is not serious. Teach this lesson when it is just you and your child, never in another's presence. Ask the child to guess what you are trying to teach him. When he finally answers with "please don't interrupt," you know you have taught a good lesson.

4. Use exchanges between ill-mannered actors on television for demonstrations. Ask "Who was rude in that program?" or "Let's count the manners mistakes." This kind of critique is proper because actors are people we don't know personally.

5. Be sure to alert your child to the times you will want him to interrupt you, such as when her brother is about to fall off the roof of the house, or his sister is trying to drown the family cat.

6. When he or she must interrupt, teach the child to say "Pardon Me" or "Excuse me" or "I am sorry, Mom, but …"

Contradicting

Contradicting and interrupting have a lot in common. Contradictions usually come as interruptions when we blurt out our opinion, which is usually the opposite point of view of the speaker. It is the same as calling someone a liar, although that is seldom our intention. Often a contradiction is an impulsive reaction. Perfecters frequently contradict someone's statement because they feel they must make sure the facts of the story are stated correctly.

Scene: Kevin: "You did not."
Thomas: "I did, too."
And so it goes until you give someone an alternative. There

is a pleasant way to disagree and get your point across. Explain that it is acceptable and sometimes necessary to disagree with someone, but it is never acceptable to be rude. We must teach our children proper ways to respond when we disagree. We must give them alternate phraseology, such as in the following scene.

Kevin: "Are you sure you said that?" or "I did not understand it that way," or "I did not hear it that way," or "I know you think you heard me say that, but I said ..."

Yelling Out

What household has not been plagued with loud outbursts? Sister yells upstairs to inform her brother that the phone call is for him. Tempers flair in family togetherness and a shouting contest ensues with each child hoping to out-shout the other. Are children the only ones who yell?

Scene: (Shouting at ten decibels) Mom: "Jimmy, stop shouting! Just be quiet!"

When she heard her voice shouting, Mom quietly suggested a game. "Let's see who can talk the quietest." She made Kevin a partner in the lesson—the quiet game.

Often we don't realize that our children get their behavior (even negative actions) from their primary models—us, their parents. The older our children grow, the more people they interact with each day. We must show them how to be respectful, responsible children.

Teaching Children to be Respectful

We use our interpersonal skills every time we interact with others. We now live and work elbow to elbow. Soon we will enter the twenty-first century with a burgeoning population. Just as we practice good personal hygiene, such as showering and using deodorant, we must bathe our children with the sweet fragrance of respect and responsibility. Good interpersonal skills attract friends to our children. Good manners and respect retain them.

Teaching Children to Show Respect

"Respect your elders" was an admonition we once heard often. We parents need to revive it. After the teachings of Sigmund Freud, Sol Gordon, John Dewey, and others, our society has emphasized self-gratification, looking out for number one, and respecting one's personal wishes. Respect for others has taken a back seat. Because our children are born with a "self" mentality, we must teach them to show respect for the feelings and needs of others. Even the *World Book Dictionary* says, "children should show respect to those who are older and wiser." The Bible says respect means "to esteem" or "honor" (Mal. 1:6).

When we show respect to our children and when they respect the needs of others over their own desires, the children gradually see how good it makes them feel—about themselves, their actions, and about others. A healthy sense of God-given self worth goes a long way in bringing out the best in us. When children feel good about themselves in light of their high value to God, they are more able to show respect for others.

Children show respect for their elders when they obey the rules that adults impose on them and when they defer to adults such as when they stand to give their seat to an adult. Another important area where children should show respect is with their peers. They must learn to share, be polite, and show consideration, letting their guests be first in the games.

Sharing with Others

It takes two or more to share. Teaching children early to share and take turns makes their first experience in the outside world more pleasant. Our job is to find alternative methods to keep children satisfied, though perhaps not happy, about the sharing.

An adult's pleasant, matter-of-fact tone of voice is crucial in diffusing the tension. Showing anger or frustration or impatience sometimes reveals favoritism. Let's look at some examples.

Scene: Two children want to play with the same toy. Instead of snatching it away from the one who has it, try to persuade one to play with something else until time to exchange. Using a kitchen timer, have the children exchange after a reasonable amount of time. Remember, five minutes feels like fifteen to the child who is waiting his turn. Short time boundaries are better for young children.

If a timer is not available, wait until one child's interest has waned and say, "It's Joel's turn now" and immediately offer something else to the child holding the toy of choice as you exchange. Create a diversion, not a crisis. If one toy catches the fancy of more than one child, we do well to insist that children take turns whether there are two children or many children playing. A three-minute egg timer with sand descending top to bottom as the seconds trickle away provides an excellent signal for very young children. They can watch the sand empty into the bottom receptacle.

Respecting the Wishes of a Guest

A child host should not attempt to force a guest playmate to play something he does not want to play. As adults we ask our guests if they would like to play Charades or Trivial Pursuit™ or some other game after dinner. As adult hosts we never coerce our guests to engage in any activity if we want our friendships to endure.

Pushing and Shoving

Children should never be permitted to push and shove. Discourage such actions by placing the pusher at the end of the line. When we consider the many lines in which our children will stand in the future, we see that early lessons in respect and fair play benefit our children throughout life.

Showing Our Rude Side

When a child is rude, make sure he knows why that behavior upsets you. Define *rude* if necessary. Other words for rude are *impolite, discourteous,* and *inconsiderate,* all of which may be just as hard for Sam or Mary to understand. Children may not understand words but they understand feelings.

Scene: Sam stares at the lady sitting next to him in church because her nose protrudes like a ski jump. If Mom scolds, "Don't be rude," Sam looks puzzled and keeps staring. Privately, Mom explains how staring makes other people feel uncomfortable, or she says, "Staring hurts others' feelings, Sam."

For deliberate acts of rudeness toward a sibling, try taking away a privilege, such as a favorite television program or a more preferred pastime activity.

Rudeness is the weak man's imitation of strength.
ERIC HOFFER

Another technique employs marbles in a jar, as discussed earlier. This time put fifty marbles or other objects in a jar. Every time little brother is rude, such as when he makes an ugly face at someone, take away a marble. Add marbles when he talks pleasantly in a situation in which he would likely have been insulting in the past. One expert recommends using tokens or coupons for a new toy or book, or one-half hour of fun, but useful, television. Sugarless candy could also be a reward.

Along with teaching respect comes teaching our children to be responsible for their own actions and reactions.

Teaching Children to be Responsible

The U.S. Department of Education reports that "Today, there is wide recognition that many of our children are not learning to act responsibly while they are young. Studies show that many children see nothing wrong with cheating on tests . . . with taking things that don't belong to them. . . . Many parents will also want to share with their children deeply held religious and moral convictions as a foundation for ethical behavior."[1]

Breaking the word *responsibility* into two parts, we see "ability to respond" or "response ability"—the ability to choose our response. A child's capacity to respond to any stimulus depends, of course, on age, coordination, maturation, information provided, and his inner needs and fears.

Other words associated with responsibility are *culpability, blame,* and *accountability.* To help an age-appropriate child learn the meaning and the spelling, tell him to remember: "I alone bear the responsibility for my own actions." The word responsibility has three i's, more than any other letter in the word.

A worthy goal in teaching responsibility is to help our children make decisions based on others' needs, not our selfish desires. It all comes down to how we feel about ourselves during or after the action. We usually feel good when we show compassion and when we do something for someone because we care and not for reward or personal gain. We must demonstrate this truth before our children.

There are three i's in responsibility.

Say to your child, "I want to show you something about responsibility. Lift your arm." After a few minutes say, "Now put your arm down. How did your arm go up? Did I, your dad, make it go up?"

The child shakes his head no. "No, Son, you raised it. If I had lifted it, I would have taken your arm and raised it. Right? Then who was responsible?"

Responsibility is a big word for a young child. He may not understand completely, but he will understand that he controls his actions and reactions. Taking responsibility is controlling our actions by our reaction.

Acting Responsibly with the Property of Others

Responsibility covers many areas, and one of them is how we treat things that belong to others.

Scene: Timmy pulls up a handful of petunias in Mrs. Smith's yard, and runs with excitement offering his gift to mom. Does she thank him or scold him or both?

Scolding may be instructive. It may prevent further uprooted bouquets, but it surely will discourage generosity and hurt the child's feelings.

Mom can thank him and explain that if all the petunias were uprooted, there would be no pretty flowers to enjoy later. She will surely talk to him about taking something that does not belong to him. She can show him how to replant them or return them to the neighbor with an explanation. (If the neighbor has a sharp tongue and guards her flower garden by threatening intruders with bodily harm, Mom may forego taking her young offender with her to apologize to Mrs. Smith.)

This mom has an opportunity to teach a valuable lesson about giving in to sudden impulses. She demonstrates that lesson by explaining that her first impulse was to scold him, but thanks him instead and explains the results of pulling up all the flowers. By doing so she encourages generosity rather than stifling it. Depending on Timmy's age, he may not understand all the nuances of that lesson, but he will absorb the gist of it. She may have to teach similar lessons often, but bringing up a "responsible" child is worth the effort.

Adults have a way of becoming attached to material objects that children do not consider important. Example: Junior punches holes in a soft drink can with Dad's new Cartier pen. To Junior they are just an old can and a tool to poke holes.

To teach a lesson here, think of something Junior does not want anyone to play with—especially his little brother who has a way of destroying things Junior loves. "How would you feel if someone tore apart your Lego™ tower that you spent hours building? Or think how you would feel if someone pulled out the tape of your favorite video. That's how Dad feels about his expensive fountain pen."

Another area of taking responsibility is admitting when we make a mistake. We all do! Some children by temperament shy away from activities and people for fear of making a mistake. A Perfecter child is an example.

Once again mom and dad pass on their manners by the way they handle their mistakes. It is not the end of the world. If the individual in error knows how to repair any damage, he is not as fearful to try out new things and to be with new people. That is one purpose of this book. A demonstration is always the best way to teach. Don't just show and tell; *show* and *involve*.

Example: Brush against your child's arm as if by accident, making him drop something—something unimportant, of course, like a pencil.

Say, "Oh, sorry about that." Picking up the pencil, check for damage and sharpen it if the lead is broken. Offer to replace the pencil if it is broken. Point out that offering to repair a mishap shows responsibility.

Prompt the Tardy

Being late seems to be epidemic in our society. We show responsibility, respect the time of others, and develop respect for ourselves when we show up on time.

Most of us know adults who never arrive on time, but even children of four or five should understand what it means to be late. It is disrespectful and makes us undependable.

In teaching teens in my classes I have had calls from parents with one specific request: teach punctuality. One mom said, "No matter how early I get my daughter up Sunday mornings, we wait for her in the car. By the time we rush down the freeway to church, our nerves are on edge, and we are shouting at one another."

How inconsiderate that daughter is, we think. Yet that young girl probably has many excuses that all satisfy her, but not her family.

Here are some things to try: (no guarantees)

- Make sure the tardy one knows what is expected. You cannot just say, "Be on time for dinner." You must make sure everyone knows what time dinner will be ready.

- Show a child how to pack and hang his or her gym bag on the doorknob the night before so he or she won't have to pack it the next morning.

- With preschool children tell them a time and then remind them fifteen minutes before the time is up if they are engrossed in play. Young children have no concept of time.

- Again, the little three-minute "sand-in-the-hourglass" timer will give young children a way to measure time that they can see. It can even challenge them to see if they can finish a task before the sand runs out.

- One parent I know uses a whistle to remind her children who are playing with friends down the street. A bell is another option—depending on how amenable the neighbors are.

- Promptness can be taught by modeling in reverse. Be late yourself with breakfast or in picking up a child from some activity, making him or her miss part of a special event or television program. Careful explanation must accompany this technique. It is not for everyone.

- Two alarm clocks screeching at different places in the child's bedroom can get a child to school on time. Perhaps you can get the teacher to work with you on a teaching project. Tell your child that he or she is responsible for getting to school on time. After he is late a few times, he may change his ways—if you're lucky. The age of a child should always be a factor in trying new techniques.

Opting for Praise and Suggestion

Praise should reinforce positive, constructive behavior. It should be highly specific rather than general. "I like the way you got ready on time today. I noticed you laid out your school clothes last night" is more specific than "You were a good boy this morning." Praise should be genuine and deserved. We should avoid empty flattery which occurs when we heap compliments on a child for something he or she has no control over. Flattery is unearned laudation and often comes across as insincere.

In addition to praise, we should give reminders before an act. Reminders and corrections after the deed carry negative messages and reap negative results. The immediate act may be corrected by a negative reprimand, but often a positive comment is better. Too many no's undermine a parent's authority. Focusing on mistakes, failures, and misdeeds discourages the desired behavior. That focus may produce hostility in the Powerful and the Perfecter children while discouraging the Phun-Lover and the Pleaser children.

Offering praise inspires our children to be respectful, to cooperate, and to take responsibility, but often it is the last thing we try, especially in the area of manners. At times we criticize and belittle children over an infraction of the rules. Children deserve our respect. We must earn theirs. Mom or Dad says, "Don't do that" when a child breaks a rule of manners. When the child stops, many of us merely cease to criticize instead of saying, "Thank you" or "That is good. You remembered to say thank you."

A child who hears only correction gets a negative picture of himself and feels discouraged and even rebellious about trying to do the mannerly thing. If all that Mom and Dad notice is bad behavior, the child thinks: *What is the use of trying?* A discouraged youngster is a sad picture. It is avoidable with appropriate praise and positive comments.

One form of praise is suggestion. Perhaps the parent cannot honestly say, "Your manners are perfect" but he or she can say, "You know, you are getting better and better at remembering your manners," or "I noticed your good manners when your present was opened last at the party today."

Suggestion works, making the parent and child partners. Suggestion will build a positive feeling in children; then they will be inspired to tailor their behavior to fit that good feeling. All personality types improve with praise, enthusiasm, and positive comments.

5

• • •

Meeting and Introducing

All people smile in the same language.

id you ever walk on a sandy beach and get a shoe full of grit? How about the sandlot at the ball park in the summer time? It has a way of bothering us so much we can't wait to get the shoe off for a good shaking to rid ourselves of the pesky irritant—for the moment anyway.

Neglecting our manners when we meet and greet people is like sand grinding our social gears to a stop. Rudeness gives others an unforgettably bad first impression of us. Abrasive behavior can lose friends and rob us of social success. First impressions are important.

We all want others to like us and our children, but with the best grades, the trendiest clothes, the latest expensive toys, and the most prestigious summer camps, our children may not know how to make new friends without some manners to oil their social gears.

To operate smoothly within the social code, we learn the rules of etiquette coupled with the good manners in our heart.

Learning the rules of etiquette
coupled with the good manners in our heart
helps us operate smoothly within the social code.

Our children need to know how to stand for their elders smile, look people in the eye, shake hands properly, and introduce themselves and others.

The importance of first impressions is not overrated. They can make or break deals of great significance. Good or bad, first impressions endure. We make a first impression in ten to twenty seconds, but it takes ten future meetings to change a bad first impression to a positive one.

Temperament, confidence, and experience all play a part in how well our children meet and greet others. Some children withdraw while others eagerly respond to any friendly face.

Does your child stand frozen when the time comes to meet and greet people? Your child may be a Pleaser or a Perfecter. They are usually less aggressive with new people than the Phun-Lovers and Powerfuls. Whatever his personality, he needs some training to build his confidence, and he needs appropriate experiences to make him feel good about meeting new people.

Equipping without Tripping

Learning can be fun. The method of instruction is the key. A classmate of mine was friendly when her parents were not around. They had nagged and preached: "Speak to people you meet. Can't you greet people with a smile and say hello? You embarrass me when you don't." My friend rebelled. Her parents never got to see her good manners, and she never heard their praise.

A fun way to learn "meeting and greeting" is to make a game of it. Books, videos, and television programs present opportunities to critique actors and characters. We seldom approve of the manners we see on television; therefore, television programs offer funny but distressing examples of poor social behavior. We can point out to our children the good and the bad manners we see, then come up with ways the television characters could improve their rude behavior.

The Five S's of Meeting Others

After seeing the need for good manners, a child needs instruction and experience. If Mom and Dad always stand, smile, look people in the eye, shake hands, and say hello, their children usually follow their lead without realizing they have learned to make a good first impression. The five S's become second nature to them—a worthy goal for all teachers and students. Practicing the five S's can mean the difference between good and bad impressions.

Stand, Smile, See, Shake, Say

Stand

Children should stand when an adult enters the room. They should stand when they are introduced to someone their own age or to someone older.

---

*If you see someone without a smile,
give them one of yours.*

Smile

Smiles are contagious. Give one and you get one in return. Smiles read the same on any face in any language. Only fourteen muscles contract to form a smile. Seventy-two muscles wrinkle into a frown.

See the Color of Their Eyes

If you feel self-conscious about looking people in the eye, look for the color of their eyes, or practice looking at yourself in the mirror until you feel comfortable doing so. If you can look yourself in the eye, you should be able to comfortably look anyone in the eye.

Try playing a game to see how long you can make eye contact with a close friend or a family member without glancing away. Choose someone who is not intimidating. Blinking is permitted. Keeping a straight face is the hardest part. Grinning widely is permitted, but if you break your concentration on the person's eyes, you lose.

Families sometimes communicate for days only by voice. Their eyes never meet. A little girl named Becky climbed into a chair next to her mom as she chopped vegetables for dinner. Her mom listened in that preoccupied way we parents do. Occasionally Mom uttered, "Umm. Is that right? Uh huh." Becky took her mom's face with her hands to gently turn it so her mom would be looking right at her. Becky wanted her mom's love—the love that only the eyes can show. When we look someone in the eye, we give them a present—ourselves. People like that.

Shake Hands

The rules for shaking hands have become somewhat blurred. Long ago, only men shook hands. Today both men and women and even children shake hands. Despite some confusion, we are all the better for the innovation. Shaking hands is a warm gesture.

Proper handshakes are:

- Firm—No one likes to palm a limp fish.
- Dry—No one likes to shake a wet hand. (Wipe it before you extend it, if necessary.)
- Not too long—Either person can release the grip first.

- Not pumped vigorously—One strong movement up and down is usually enough, but a longer, stronger handshake is not improper.
- Not crushing—Among the people who plead for gentleness are those with an arthritic or crippled hand, and those wearing rings.
- Right handed—Most people shake hands with their right hand. Individuals with a disabled right hand may extend their left hand to able persons who grasp the extended left hand with their right or left hand. Our U.S. Senator Robert Dole from Kansas sets that example. He has a war injury which precludes the use of his right hand; yet he shakes thousands of hands each year using his left hand. We often see him on television news programs grasping a pen in his right hand which is permanently drawn in that position. I think he carries the pen to let people see that he will not be extending his right hand. Politics aside, his success and affability set a good example for parents to use with a disabled child.

The Perfect Handshake. Two people grasp right hands. With the thumb raised we form a "v" between our thumb and forefinger. The "v's" of each hand should meet.

If you choose not to shake hands for any reason, say, "I'm sorry I can't shake your hand." Immediately engage the person in conversation so he or she will not feel the sting of what might be perceived as your rejection. You may also keep your hands out of sight, maybe behind your back to let others know you do not shake hands.

Women and Men. Both sexes shake hands the same way. Women do not turn their hand palm down. The hand-kissing custom died with petticoats and bloomers.

Some of the following questions about handshakes are often asked in my classes or newspaper column. (1) Do women shake hands with other women? Yes. We see that more often in the business world than in social activities, but extending our hand to another woman is a polite gesture any time. (2) Who should extend a hand first—the man or the woman? The answer is that either sex may extend a hand first. However—and that is a big "however" in some circles—men once learned to extend their hand only when the lady offered hers first. (The reason is in appendix C, p. 195, but that rule no longer endures!)

In my classes I teach males to observe the old rule in formal social situations, such as wedding receptions, funerals, private parties, and the like. A good rule of thumb is: If you have doubts, let the lady extend her hand first. Similarly, I strongly urge all females to make it a practice to shake hands. After they become accustomed to it, they find that it is far better than just standing there exchanging hellos. It gives us something to do.

Say Hello

The next "S" is Say hello, and always say the person's name if you know it. To show respect, children should use a title and the last name such as "Hello, Mr. Kendall." If Mr. Kendall prefers, he may tell the child to call him Charlie, but parents have the final say about how their children address adults.

After "Hello, Mrs. Bemis," we can add a phrase such as, "I'm happy to meet you," or "I have heard good things about you." Don't say, "I have heard a lot about you." That leaves the person wondering, *good things or bad?* A rule of thumb for titles and first names between two adults is: If you are in doubt, use a title and their last name. Then if they prefer that we use their first name, adults should honor their wish, no matter their age.

Prepare ahead by telling your child to use the name of the person that you give to him when you introduce him to someone.

Example: Mom sees her friend, Alicia, in the grocery store. Mom says, "Alicia, I want to introduce my son, Gary, to you. Gary, this is Mrs. Overstreet." Gary says, "Hello, Mrs. Overstreet." Mom calls her friend Alicia, but she wants her son to call her Mrs. Overstreet.

Sometimes children must introduce themselves. They follow the first four S's: *Stand, Smile, See the eyes, Shake hands,* and say "My name is_____(first and last names)" or "Hi, I am_____(first and last names)." They can add a phrase such as "I am Sandra and Hank Gould's daughter."

When parting, each person says "I am glad to have met you," or "It was nice meeting you," or a similar phrase.

Teaching the Five S's

Children learn the rules of meeting and greeting slowly and over time. We must teach them patiently and consistently by example and instruction. When we first begin teaching the five S's, we do well to visualize a friend forcing the five S's on us—for our own good, of course. Seeing such a picture in our mind, we feel the discomfort we impose on our children if we demand a perfect performance.

Demonstrating slowly we make it a game by having two children observe and guess the five S's as we show them the steps. After both children act out all five S's, let them critique their performances. If the game is still fun, repeat it once for practice. When the fun ceases, save that game (lesson) for another day.

I use this method with students of all ages with good results, but if teaching the five S's seems a little formal for your taste, teach the rules and let the children suggest ways to adapt them to their personality. For instance, "hi" will suit a Phun-Lover. The Perfecter may choose the more formal "hello."

Teach the common sense exceptions of standing for adults. For example, when an adult enters the room, children should stand unless doing so is disruptive. When the school teacher reenters the room, children remain seated.

In our homes the decision is clearer. When an adult enters a room for the first time, a child guest stands to meet and greet that adult. (Adult guests should stand to meet others, also.)

The Importance of Proper Introductions

Learning how to stand, smile, see their eyes, shake hands, and say hello makes a good first impression. We also want to introduce people properly and to respond appropriately when we are introduced. We like people who remember to introduce us. Did you ever feel out of place standing in a group with your friend who talked to the person next to you whom you did not know? (If that happens, just introduce yourself. Wait for a pause and say, "My name is Misty Baxter. I don't think I have met you.")

Making introductions is sharing a present, a friend's name, with another friend or acquaintance. We all feel more comfortable around new people when we have a name to use when speaking to them. It also gives us pleasure to share our friends with others. One way we do that is by exchanging our friends' names. That is all that introductions are. Many times people neglect introducing others because they are afraid of the rules—rules they have never learned.

Long ago, English teachers taught students how to make proper introductions. The only place our children learn today is by watching and learning from us. How important is it? Knowing how to introduce people properly can go a long way in building our confidence and increasing our influence with others— spiritually, socially, and professionally. To be "in favor with man," we must know how to introduce ourselves and others. Afraid of making mistakes, people often pretend to "just forget" to make introductions. Neglecting to introduce people is worse than breaking some rules in trying. Introducing people properly requires some rules, but the rules are not our enemy. They make it possible for us to show deference to others out of respect.

Socially, we give females, our elders, and dignitaries the most respect, regardless what we think of them. In business, rank (seniority) is the criterion. Another name for it is the "pecking order." Generally, in business affairs we introduce an entry-level individual to an executive, regardless the age or sex. Generally, we honor the customer over a business associate, even our boss. Our focus will be on the social rules.

The single most important rule
of making introductions is to make the attempt,
even if you forget the rules and the names.

Learning the Basics of Introductions

1. Introduce a male to a female.
2. Introduce a younger person to an older person.
3. Introduce a less important person to a more important person.

Those are the basic rules stated in all etiquette books, but notice the phrase "introduce . . . to" That puts the first emphasis on the less important person. I find that confusing.

You already have questions, don't you? I will try to answer them after we get the basics. Complications arise because it is sometimes hard to determine who is more important; for example, an elderly male rabbi and a young female governor. (Choose the rabbi.)

If you practice this plan consistently, I can almost promise that you will soon be making introductions with confidence. Here is a simple pattern that I have taught with success for many years.

1. Decide which person is more important.
2. Look at Mr. Important and say the first name (or title)

and last name. "Dr. Alred, this is Andy Carlson, a classmate of mine."

3. Turn and say, "Andy, this is Dr. Alred, my biology professor."

Notice: You did not use the words *introduce you to* in either scene.

If you prefer to say "introduce you to," you must begin with the less important person. "Andy, I'd like to introduce you to Dr. Alred." The little words *introduce to* make the crucial difference. Sometimes, it is easier to start with the less important person. Perhaps in the scene above Andy has just walked up to you and Dr. Alred. As you greet Andy, you introduce him; therefore, you begin with him, the less important, and you use "introduce you to." Remember, we are not talking about importance in the sense of whom we like better.

I suggest you always follow the first plan and start with the more important person until you are comfortable making introductions.

Rule of Thumb: A man is almost never honored as more important over a woman unless he is of royal blood, a high church official, a much older gentleman, or a head of state.

Rule of Thumb: We love our family, but as a courtesy we treat those outside our family as more important when we make introductions. "Coach Greenfelt, this is my grandfather, Dr. Adamson." This is a gray area in etiquette books. You may prefer to honor the grandfather.

Another example is "Clay, this is my mom, Mrs. Harding." If you start with Mom, you must use the phrase "introduce you to." "Mom, I want to introduce you to my friend, Clay."

Responding Properly

The rules for responding to an introduction are fairly simple. Any polite greeting, such as hello, will do as long as you repeat the name of the new acquaintance. Repeating the name helps us remember it, and people like for us to remember their name. "I am happy to meet you, Professor Alred."

Always repeat the name of the person introduced to you.

Those are the basic rules for making introductions, but a few remain that we need to know.

- Speak the names distinctly so that each name is clearly heard by the person who needs it. So often we repeat someone's name to their face instead of giving it to the person who needs it. We look at the person whose name we are trying to remember. We are nervous, and we mumble. We have a gift to give (the name), and we should face the person receiving the gift. For new learners that may be a distant goal.
- We should always give last names along with titles or first names: Jennifer Johnson or Dean Shoemaker or my grandmother, Mrs. Braer. The new acquaintance may feel uncomfortable calling your grandmother Nanna. Your friend will call her Mrs. Braer.
- Children should state a parent's last name if it is different. Alan Orr says, "This is my mom, Kay Poe."
- When introducing someone to a small group, say the name of the newcomer first. For example, "Mary Briley, these are my friends from church: Amber, Ray, Molly, and Brent." Last names are not necessary with so many people because Mary will use first names with her peers.
- When introducing someone to a large group, get the crowd's attention and say, "I want to introduce my

friend, Mary Briley, from church. Please introduce yourself to her later."

- Children should be introduced, not ignored. They deserve the respect. As soon as a child is talking, we should introduce them to others just as we would an adult. We ask a child to respond with the name we give him. He may not be able to say "Hello, Mrs. Barnes" very plainly, but we have begun the learning process.

Making Self-Introductions

Always be prepared to introduce yourself. Your host at a party may be too busy to do the honors, or he or she may not know how.

In another situation the friend standing next to you may forget to introduce you. Just smile, make eye contact, put out your hand, and say hello or "Hi, I'm James Collier."

Now for the big question students always ask before I even begin teaching the rules of making introductions.

The "What Ifs" in Introductions

Forgetting and Mispronouncing Names

What if my mental computer crashes, and I can't even remember by sister's name, much less my second-grade classmate who moved away years ago and is now standing next to me waiting to be introduced? We all forget names occasionally, even our own. No one I know is immune to that embarrassment.

Hint: Repeating a name after you hear it and using it in the subsequent conversation is the best insurance against forgetfulness.

Choosing First Names or Last Names

If in doubt, use the last name of the person you are meeting. He can always say, "Please call me Charlie," and she can say, "Please call me Mary."

Finessing the Name

There are at least three options open to us when our mind just goes blank. We must make an attempt to introduce others.

1. One method is to introduce yourself to the person approaching you. Even if the person already knows your name, he will probably state his (you hope). "Hi, I'm Alan Decker." Alan hopes to hear the reciprocal, "Hi, I'm Jerry Kemp." If Jerry remembers Alan, but sees a puzzled look on Alan's face, it is helpful for Jerry to say something about himself, such as where he and Alan met.

2. The second option is to ignore the rule about who is more important and just say the only name you can remember, hoping the other person will introduce himself. For example, when you remember only one name, just say, "Meet my associate, Ann Watts" and hope the friend whose name escapes you introduces himself or herself.

3. When all other options run out, we must admit we have gone blank and make some excuse about forgetfulness. People understand that better than bad manners, such as pretending to "just forget" to make the introductions.

What if you don't understand the name when you are introduced to someone? Say, "I didn't get your name," or "Could you repeat your name, please?"

What if someone mispronounces your name? Correct them once. Perhaps your name is Jane and the new acquaintance says, "Hi, Jean." Say, "It's Jane." It is kinder to correct the error once than let the person call you by the wrong name all evening and later learn of his or her mistake.

The rules become extremely important when we need to show deference to or respect for certain people. For that reason our children should be taught the rules with our gentle instruction and modeling as we show respect to others. Everyone deserves the respect of an introduction and the gift of a name to call someone.

So far, I have explained the basics rules and some "what ifs." Now, we will look at how to teach our children.

Teaching Our Children How to Make Introductions

Presenting a Gift-Wrapped Package
- A gift-wrapped package makes a good teaching aid.
- Invite a friend over to play a game with your child.
- Demonstrate with the package that you have wrapped. Follow the rules and introduce the children by presenting the package at the same time you say a name. The proper response is simple: "It's nice to meet you." But the two children may say anything appropriate for the situation.
- Then let your child introduce you to the guest. Your child holds the gift-wrapped package which represents mom's name and presents it to her friend as she says, "Jenny, this is my mom, Mrs. Kendricks. Mom, this is Jenny Wilder."

Wearing Hats as Props
Hats also make good props for teaching deference to children. Pretend that one child is the coach. Place a coach's hat or ball cap on his or her head to show that the coach is more important than the student.

"Coach, this is my friend Katie Grover from out of town."

Turn and say, "Katie, this is Coach Simmons, our soccer coach." Although Katie is female, the coach is older and more distinguished.

Practicing Makes Proper

- "Suzie, this is my grandmother, Mrs. Hester. Grandma, meet Suzie Wilson from my fifth period class." Why all the names? Most of us have at least two grandmothers. Blended families may have eight. Suzie needs to know what to call Grandma.

- "Mrs. Edmondson, this is my father, Paul Jacobs. Dad, this is Michael Farrar's mom, Mrs. Edmondson." Remember, children and parents don't always have the same last name. Dad will be embarrassed if he says, "Hello, Mrs. Farrar" and later learns about his mistake.

Scene: The new school year is underway. Mom has met Karen's teacher, but Dad has not. Open house will provide a good opportunity for young Karen to practice making introductions.

If Karen's parents wait until they arrive and say to her, "Aren't you going to introduce us to your teacher?" they relieve their own embarrassment, but poor Karen will feel embarrassed and awkward. Making us as parents look good is not nearly as important as protecting Karen's feelings.

A few days before open house Mom or Dad practices with Karen. The scene might play out like this:

Mom says, "Karen, when we get to your classroom you can introduce Dad to Mrs. Abernathy. Let's practice."

Choose a time when Karen appears to be in the mood. Tell her how good you will both feel when she introduces you.

Mom says, "When we get to the school, Karen, you can say, 'Mrs. Abernathy, this is my dad, James Kirkus.'"

Finding a Remedy for Complications

Perhaps the scene plays out this way. Mom and Karen have practiced, but when they get to school Karen suddenly changes from the magpie in the car to the cat that lost its meow. What is a parent to do after all that planning and teaching?

Karen's feelings are more important than any lesson. She will be easily embarrassed in front of her teacher. So, after seeing that Karen either forgets or fears making the introduction, Mom looks at the teacher and says, "Hello, I am Emily Kirkus, Karen's mom. We met before the beginning of school. This is Karen's dad, James Kirkus." Mom gestures toward Dad.

Dad waits for Mrs. Abernathy to extend her hand. If she does, he shakes her hand and says, "It is nice to meet you, Mrs. Abernathy."

By not mentioning what may be obvious to Karen—that she "messed up"—Mom and Dad show her that she is more important than the lesson on introductions. There will be many more opportunities to practice introducing people.

Making It Easier to Introduce People

- Take a deep breath, take your time, and decide who is more important.
- Remember that importance has nothing to do with character or your preference. It has to do with age, sex, and position.
- If it is more practical to address the less important person first, remember to use the phrase "introduce you to."
- Exchange the names for the new acquaintances.
- If you forget all the rules and all the names, just admit it, but don't neglect to at least try to introduce one friend to another. Say something like "My mind has gone blank. Help me out and introduce yourselves." (This is the least desirable option, but it is better than ignoring the introduction.)
- Choose a phrase and stick to it until making introductions becomes easier. "This is" is the safest one.

- Finally, remember that lapses of memory haunt us all. Letitia Baldrige was the social secretary during President Kennedy's administration. She tells amusing stories of her own faux pas. Once she introduced a husband and wife to one another! I think I have made all the mistakes at one time or another, but I keep trying. Introducing people is that important.

Providing Opportunities to Meet and Introduce

- Watching and discussing television programs together
- Reading books together
- School activities
- Church functions
- Reunions with relatives, perhaps, during the holidays
- Chance meetings with business colleagues
- When old or new friends come to visit
- When playmates come over

6

· · ·

From Toy Phones to Cell Phones

Kindness is a language the deaf can hear and the blind can see.

Voice mailboxes, car phones, cordless telephones that hide from us, and answering machines that play tag—all burdens or blessings, depending on our perspective. Now there are telephones that beam images to us over the lines. We can only imagine what will happen when our kids start watching the telephone as well as "hogging" it.

The telecommunications experts have brought us a long way from telephones that had a crank on the side for ringing up the operator who plugged a wire into the number on the switchboard. Alexander Graham Bell invented the technology for instant communication, giving us a life-saving tool that connects us to the world. Little did he know the woes we would create for ourselves with his invention, not to mention the manners transgressions.

Somehow it seems easier for rudeness to thrive when we can't see the perpetrator.

If children remain uneducated in the niceties of telephone etiquette, they will unknowingly carry bad telephone habits into adulthood. At one time children were formally taught the few rules we needed. Today telephone manners or the lack of them are not so much taught as absorbed, and we need far more rules because of the new devices and added features. Early training and parents who model proper behavior on the telephone are what we need. Consider the following scenario played out every evening over the phone lines.

"Hey, is Danny around?" comes a voice from a noisy background. Danny's dad calmly responds, "Danny cannot come to the telephone at the moment."

"Don't you have a portable phone you can take to him?"

Dad tries again, "Danny can't come to the phone. Would you like to leave a message?"

"Uh." Click! Dial toooone.

The voice on the other end of the line is probably from a very nice, but untutored, young caller. We can hardly blame all the manners violations on the young. Trainers in business offices struggle to correct this annoying problem among employees every day.

Returning rude for rude is not the answer. It's up to us as parents to train our children in good telephone habits. Often, we make our first and sometimes our only impression with someone over the telephone lines. For instance, our children will someday make such an impression when they call to set up a job interview.

Whatever their temperament, children are usually eager to talk on the telephone, perhaps first with Grandma while Mom or Dad makes the call and holds the receiver. To gain telephone privileges as they get older, they are more interested in learning the rules of telephone etiquette than they are in proper dining skills. Phun-Loving children especially seem to be born with "phone genes."

When to Begin Teaching Telephone Manners

Children mature at different rates; therefore, I feel parents know better than anyone when a child is ready. Our three-year-old granddaughter can recite her telephone number, but does not punch in the numbers on the phone pad. The telephone remains out of reach.

Toy phones give young children a chance to pretend to talk, but the real phone should not be used as a toy. It can be dangerous. An article on child safety in *Parents* magazine says we should keep the telephone out of a youngster's reach. A baby might hurt himself with the cord, and if a toddler knocks the receiver off, he or she may be frightened by the beeping.[1]

A child of four or five should not be screening calls. A young child who can punch a preprogrammed key or the number one on the key pad and ten other digits can give parents unwanted long-distance charges. The preprogrammed keys are very convenient for us and perhaps too convenient for young children if the telephone is accessible.

Begin training in the basics as early as you feel they are ready. Dialing 911 or 0 may be your first choice if you leave your child with a baby-sitter. You may choose to begin with how to answer the telephone properly, then how to make a call, and how to handle the added features such as call-waiting, call forwarding, and answering machines.

The Basics of Telephone Etiquette

Answering Properly

Some families answer their telephone with "Hello. The Jamison residence." Other parents prefer a safer response because all callers are unknown unless we subscribe to a caller ID service.

The safest response is a simple "Hello" or "Hello, this is 555-0000." It is not necessary to identify yourself when answering your home telephone. A stranger has intruded until he or she gives you a name.

These are the essentials to teach family members about answering the telephone:

- Answer with a smile. The person on the other end can hear a smile in your voice. To demonstrate that in both my adult and children's classes, I have a student turn away from the group and say something without smiling, and then say the same thing with a smile. The audience can always detect the difference without seeing the student's face.
- It is not rude to ask a caller's name if the person on the other end of the line does not identify himself or herself. Say, "may I ask who's calling?" or "who is calling, please?"
- Do not eat, drink, or chew gum because sounds are magnified over the telephone.
- Listen carefully so you can call the person by name in the conversation.
- If a telephone call comes for another family member, do not yell to get his or her attention. Press the hold button, or put the telephone receiver down gently, and find that person.
- Family members should respect others' privacy on the telephone.
- Remind siblings they will want the same respect when they are talking on the phone.

Taking Messages

Always keep a pad and pencil near the phone. For a minimum of information, write down a caller's first and last names and a phone number.

- If the family member is not home, ask the caller if you may take a message. Say, "Patrick is not here. Would you like to leave him a message?" Write down the information and repeat it to the caller to make sure you heard everything correctly. Each family should have a central place for messages to be left.
- If the child is too young to write down a complete message, he may verbally repeat it to a caregiver. However, many messages are lost that way.

With long distance calls, a child may learn to say, "My sitter says Mom will be back about 4:00 this afternoon." That way, the caller knows the child is not alone. Also, the caller can be responsible for calling back.

Making a Call

Always consider the time before making a call. Calls should not be made at mealtime nor after 9:00 P.M. (unless prearranged).

- Announce to your family members that you will be using the telephone.
- Dial the number and identify yourself immediately when someone answers on the other end of the line. Say, "This is Joey Abernathy." It is rude not to give your name unless you are such a frequent caller you are sure the person answering will recognize your voice.

Always identify yourself immediately when making a telephone call.

- If you recognize the voice of Patrick's mom who answers the phone, speak to her with "Hello, Mrs. Evans. This is Joey. May I speak to Patrick?"

- After Patrick takes the telephone receiver, ask if this is a convenient time to talk. "Can you talk now, Patrick?"
- Always end a conversation with good-bye. The caller says good-bye first, signaling that he or she is hanging up. (Exception: A salesperson always hangs up last out of courtesy, and only after he or she makes sure all the customer's questions and requests are satisfied.)

Interrupting Others' Calls

As soon as Mom begins using the phone, it seems, the older child yells on his way toward the door, "OK if I run down to the video store? Thanks, Mom!" He bounds out the door before Mom can respond with "Not until your chores are done." Our children know how to catch us in a compromising situation.

Then there are other interruptions. As soon as Mom gets an answer on the other end of the line, two or more of the children may get into a scrape over whose turn it is to feed the dog or take out the trash. Before placing a call, Mom may suggests the kids play a game. She tells them she will be talking on the telephone. She gives them an estimate of how long she will be talking, and she tries to stay within the time limit. Young children have no concept of time. When I left my children with a sitter, I used to space my fingers or my hands apart to let them know I would not be gone long. "Just a little while," I indicated with my fingers or hands.

From a child's point of view, the phone takes up too much of a parent's time. For young children, it can even become anthropomorphic—a live competitor for their attention. That is one reason callers should always ask even close friends if they can talk at that time. We can't know their schedule or the needs of their family at the moment unless we ask if they have a few minutes.

Talking to Machines

We tend to hate or love these devices. Speaking into a recorder intimidates some callers. They do offer us real conveniences, giving callers a chance to leave a message and the owner an opportunity to be away from the telephone and still know who is trying to reach him. Along with these amenities, however, come some rules.

The outgoing message should be as brief as possible and give the necessary information. For safety reasons it is not necessary to give your name or to say you are not at home. The message most recommended is, "You have reached 555-0000. Please leave your name, number, and brief message after the tone."

You may add that you will return the call as soon as possible. Of course, that means you must return all the calls that come. We should make every effort to return our calls within twenty-four hours.

Outgoing messages should be succinct. It is not necessary to tell the caller you are unavailable; that is obvious. The message should never be "cute" or contain jargon the caller may not understand. It is annoying to have to listen to a song before we can leave our message. Long, outgoing messages are time wasters and cost long-distance callers unnecessarily.

One convenience that answering machines afford us is the ability to spend time with our family in the evening. The machine can record the calls, and we can return them after we put the children to bed. Precious time spent with our children who grow so quickly may be more important than chatting to a friend about a committee meeting or with a business partner about personal problems. Some conversations can wait a while.

Handling Call-Waiting Interruptions

A most convenient, but often annoying, feature is call-waiting. Without rules we offend callers who have no control over the nuisance, except to hang up on us.

When we hear a beep signaling us that someone else is trying to reach our telephone number, we must ask and receive permission from the first caller before we answer the call-waiting beep. Why wait for permission? The first caller may prefer to call us back to being placed on hold. The first caller takes priority.

If the phone rings while we wait for an important call, we should tell the present caller the circumstances so that when the expected call comes, we may excuse ourself, telling the first caller we will call them back. Here are some more rules:

- The call-waiting beep may be left unanswered.
- If a call comes in for Mom, a child should tell the adult caller she will get her mom to the phone. She then goes back to her friend on the first call to explain that she will call the friend back. Then she gets Mom to the phone.
- When answering call-waiting, spend as little time as possible away from the first caller.
- Tell the second caller that you are on another line and ask the caller if you may return the call. Ask the caller to name a convenient time. Then return to the prior caller.

Forwarding Calls

Alert your host that you may receive calls while you are there. The owner of the telephone will be the one who must answer all the phone calls. Never tie up another's phone with lengthy calls.

Terminating Those Beeping Signals

Many professional people today must wear a beeper at all times. Beepers should never be worn to make someone feel important. Those wearing beepers should turn off the insistent and irritating noise as quickly as possible. Or better yet, switch to a silent, vibrating signal that is now available.

Calling to and from Cellular Phones

All calls made and received on telephones in cars and those carried personally are expensive and are charged to the owner. This knowledge must be taught to our children because they ride in car pools and with parents of other friends. Personal cellular and car cellular telephones should not be used for fun. Children should always ask permission before using another's telephone, whether in their home or in their car.

Another difference between cellular phones and most other phones is that users are broadcasting with no privacy. These phones operate from cells, not over the telephone lines.

Now that we have the basics, let's look at ways to train our children for using the telephone.

Teaching Our Children How to Use the Phone

Modeling Manners

As we have already seen with other social skills, modeling is the easiest and perhaps the most effective method. Our children imitate our social skills or the lack of them. For example, if a parent hangs up when reaching a wrong number without explaining the error to the caller, children may do the same.

When we make a call our family hears us say, "This is Mrs. Delaney, may I speak to your mom if she is not busy?"

As we finish a call, our family notices if we say thank you for the information, if we say good-bye or just hang up, if we slam down the receiver or replace it gently.

Our children pick up on the tone of voice we take with callers such as solicitors. If we carelessly slam the telephone receiver down, children may do the same. And what about white lies such as the parent in the recliner who says, "Tell whoever it is that I am in the shower?" Our manners and our morals are on display when the telephone rings. Our children mirror us.

Playing Roles

Another easy way to teach phone manners is to role play the rules after you instruct. Let your child be the adult and you be the child. That way she gets to correct the parent.

In the practice session, explain the lesson to both children. If Dad is not home, the caller should not be given that information. The responses "He is unavailable" or "He is busy at the moment" are not lies.

If your child likes to learn in a group, invite some friends over for a "read the script" party. I have used these in my classes for young children for many years. Most of them love playacting.

A parent and two children will interact. Fill in the blanks.

Teaching "in Case of Emergency"

Teach children to call for help in crises. Have a plan and teach it to your children. It could mean the difference in a quick, calm response and a panic response to an emergency.

Children often learn to say their names at an early age and often can recite their address. Memorizing their home telephone number is easier for most of them than dialing it.

Another type emergency is when your four-year-old is home with the baby-sitter who suddenly becomes ill and faints. According to Sam Sebastion, Ed.D., professor of education at the University of Washington, some children as young as three can learn to cope with an emergency. Here are some tips for preparing a young child to handle an emergency.

- You can paint the "0" with a dab of red nail polish. To practice, tape the dial-tone button down and show him or her how to push the red "0."
- If you have 911 in your area, parents can teach young children those three numbers by using some nail polish or a preprogrammed number.

Practicing Telephone Scripts
Telephone Script Role Play

A parent rings a bell:	Ring, Ring.
First Child:	Hello.
Second Child:	Hi. This is _____.
	May I speak to_____
	(the first child's name).
First Child:	This is_____
	(first child's name).
Second Child:	I am calling to see if
	you know our assignment.
First Child:	Yes, it is on page twenty.
Second Child:	Thanks, I'll see you at school
	tomorrow. Good-bye.
First Child:	Good-bye.

Receiving Calls When Parents Are Away

Teacher/Parent rings a bell:	Ring, Ring.
First Child:	Hello.
Second Child:	Hi. This is_____
	(second child says his or her
	name.) Is your dad home?
First Child:	He can't come to the phone.
	May I take a message?
	(There is no need to lie
	to be safe.)
Second Child:	Thank-you. I will call back.

Receiving Calls When Parents Are Home

Teacher/Parent rings a bell:	Ring, Ring.
First Child:	Hello.
Second Child:	Is your mom or dad home?
First Child:	May I ask who is calling?
Second Child:	This is _____
	(the second child's name).

- By the age of five or six, children can describe a problem to a telephone operator. They can learn to say, "I need help" or "my baby-sitter is ill." Practice again and again. Periodically schedule refresher drills.
- Teach your child to leave the receiver off the phone when he or she is calling for help. Frequently, children hang up too quickly before the emergency person can get enough information.
- If you have automatic dialing, you can program a telephone with emergency numbers instead of painting the "0" with nail polish.

Saving Lives "In Case of Fire"

Fire departments across the country recommend that parents teach children that the telephone should not be used in a fire emergency. They should call out to others in the house, get outside, and go to a neighbor for help.

A frightened child should not have to decide whether to call the police, or the hospital, or the fire department. He or she must have the necessary information with few choices—911 or "0" or a programmed number. Make it easy. Make it clear. Practice.

When there is a fire with parents at home, make an escape plan and practice it often. Parents must plan which parent will be responsible for which child, especially at night. Without a plan a parent may come outside thinking the other parent has the child. Recently I heard of a young mother who lost her life because she went back inside the front door to get a four-year-old who had gone out the back door with her dad.

Examining the Temperament

Gender rather than temperament may reveal your child's telephone personality. Girls often like to talk on the phone more than guys.

The following are characteristics of each temperament you may see:

The Pleaser child usually speaks with a low-energy voice. These children often let someone else rush to answer the telephone. To help them improve the quality and animation of their telephone voice, record the Pleaser's voice and let him or her listen. Surprised to hear the lack of enthusiasm, the Pleaser child may begin speaking with more energy. Often these children are unaware they speak differently from others.

The Powerful child may be curt and unresponsive on the telephone. The tape recorder can help correct that behavior, also.

The Phun-Lover children are usually the first ones to grab the telephone and the ones who are "always on the phone." They love to talk.

The Perfecter likes long conversations with close friends.

If you have a large family, the telephone probably rings almost continually. I had some students from a family of six children and two parents. They said no one in the family wanted to answer the telephone. That surprised me knowing it was a house full of teens. They explained that the chances were just too great that the call would be for another family member. In a family that large or in any family with long-winded phone users, you may want to get a timer or similar tool to monitor the length of each user's call.

Whatever our child's personality and whatever added features we subscribe to, telephone manners beg to be taught. You may choose to post a short list of rules near the phone until everyone in the family who uses the telephone masters them before putting up a new list. The best way to train is to model politeness. If we teach our children good telephone manners when they are young, think of the benefits to them throughout their lives.

7

· · ·

The Perfect Guest/ The Gracious Host

I say to every man among you

not to think more highly of himself than he ought.

Romans 12:3,13

Freddie received precious few invitations for overnight visits with friends. His older sisters, Katie and Susan, often stayed over with friends. Mom knew there was a problem. There had to be a reason. Freddie invited his buddies to spend the night in his new tent in the backyard. The guys frolicked and laughed. There was the usual rowdiness with little sleep, but no one returned Freddie's invitation.

"He makes so much trouble." Susan exclaimed when Mom talked to the girls about her concerns and Freddie's obvious discouragement.

Katie chimed in, "He's bossy and always wants his own way."

"Now girls, he's only seven," Mom defended.

But Mom knew the girls were right. Freddie was old enough to know how to behave on an overnight stay at a friend's house. Mom and the girls knew that belittling Freddie would only tear down his confidence and worsen the problem. If he did not feel good about himself, he would never be interested in changing his behavior. How could they get a message to him without turning him off, destroying their chances to correct a bad situation?

The Plan

One evening at dinner the girls discussed plans for an upcoming slumber party at a friend's house. They discussed what made some parties fun and other parties boring.

"I just hate it when someone is a know-it-all and has to be the leader in every game," Katie offered.

"And I don't like it when someone complains about everything, even the food. It is so embarrassing, especially if the mom hears it," Susan said.

Dad listened to all the observations and then suggested they list traits that make someone a welcome guest.

"Freddie, will you help us? You can give us the male viewpoint," Susan glanced Freddie's way for the first time. "Then we can put it on the computer."

When Freddie heard his name, he came alive. "Yeah, I guess," he muttered, trying to hide his enthusiasm. Mom was thinking: *If I had suggested a list, Freddie would have dismissed it as just another one of those grown-up chores.*

While Katie went for pencil and paper, Freddie blurted out the first rule: Be sure to eat what the mom cooks. Katie began to write and other rules came fast, as each child named one.

The Check List
- Help with the chores.
- Go along with what the group wants to do even if it isn't your favorite game.

- Don't beg to stay longer when it is time to go.
- Don't make noise, getting on the parents' nerves.
- If you make a mess, tell the parent and help him or her clean.

(For a complete list see page 90).

The Long-Awaited Invitation

After they completed the list, Mom began to wonder how she could get an invitation for Freddie. She remembered keeping a neighbor's children overnight when the mother went to the hospital to have her baby. Several times, Mrs. Anderson had offered to return the favor. So Freddie's mom talked to the neighbor, and without mentioning the list, she arranged for Freddie to visit the Andersons the next Friday evening.

The next day an excited young man flew through the back door with an announcement. "Mrs. Anderson asked me to come stay over Friday night. She even wants me to eat dinner with them, Mom!"

Later when Freddie started packing, Katie suggested they get the "Being a Welcome Guest" list off the computer. Susan retrieved it, and Freddie checked off the needed items on the "remember to take" part of the list as he packed each one.

The Glowing Report

After the Friday evening had come and gone, Freddie's mom talked with Mrs. Anderson when they met on the front walkway picking up their newspapers one morning. Mrs. Anderson glowed with comments about Freddie's behavior.

"Freddie was a perfect gentleman. He rushed around to help put up the baseball equipment and even made his bed the next morning. He was so polite. As I served the beef stroganoff, Freddie said, 'Um, that smells delicious.' He even ate most of his serving."

The neighbor was curious about the change in Freddie. She remembered him to be a difficult little guest. Mom told her about the list of rules. Of course, Mrs. Anderson wanted to borrow the list. Freddie's mom agreed to share it, but suggested that making the list was part of the magic.

Creating a List with Your Child

Your child is unique, so be creative. Consider what will work with your child. If he or she is a list maker, as many Perfecters are, just provide pencil and paper and name the project. If he balks at the rules in general, let the idea for a list come from him or someone he admires. In other words, look for a felt need and fill it. The Phun-Lover wants social approval. They do not like lists and charts. Appeal to the Phun-Lover's desire to become a polite guest so he will get many invitations to visit friends. The Powerful wants power. The Perfecter likes organization and self-improvement. The Pleaser likes doing things with others.

Another list might include traits you and your child like to see in friends when you invite them for a slumber party. Or make a list of negatives you have seen in guests you have entertained. Sometimes a child can critique the behavior of others more easily than his own. Warning: Everyone must agree not to mention names outside the family.

Involve the children in the plan and return invitations should follow.

Freddie's Next Excursion

Soon, Freddie received an invitation to spend the weekend with Jason Smith, his friend at school. The Smith family had a well-equipped recreation room, a Nintendo™ game, and a big screen television. Outside the children swam and jumped on the trampoline. Freddie was so excited.

He was glad his mom had taught him good table manners because he knew the Smiths' large family had a big Sunday dinner.

The Fine-Tuned Plan

- Say hello to the friend's mom when you arrive.
- Obey without arguing.
- Be agreeable about the choice of activities.
- If you are hungry, ask if you may have a snack. Don't sneak it.
- At meals, eat what you can. Taste of everything, and don't say you hate the broccoli.
- Treat their possessions with respect and reasonable care.
- Be careful to wait your turn to speak, not interrupting the adults.
- Be neat and keep your things together.
- Put your dirty clothes in the plastic bag you are taking with you.
- Make your bed each morning.
- Hang up your wet towels. (Some families expect you to use your towel more than once.)
- Respect the privacy of others. Don't snoop in drawers or closets.
- Close cabinet doors and drawers.
- Before you leave, check to see that you are not leaving something the host family must return to you.
- Before leaving, be sure to thank the parents for inviting you.
- Write a thank-you note when you get home.

This weekend Jason's big brother, Tom, would be home from college. That meant a feast in the dining room, and Freddie would need to be careful how he ate.

Finally, Friday arrived. Freddie packed his bag to be ready when Jason's dad came to pick him up. Freddie's mom wanted to go over some reminders about being a gracious house guest but she waited until he finished packing. Mom did not frustrate him while he busily put his things in his gym bag. She did not preach, making Freddie feel bad about gaffes he had made in the past. She sat eye to eye with him so he could think about what she was saying. No matter how young the child is, he is due such courtesy.

Freddie's mom told him a funny story about her first overnight visit. She was playing chase in a friend's house and knocked over a huge flower pot spilling dirt all over the floor. Memories of how embarrassed and afraid she felt were still vivid. Her friend's mom was nice about the calamity. Together they cleaned up the mess, but after all these years Mom could remember how awful she felt at the time. She never ran in the house again.

"Now, Mom, I'm ready," Freddie announced. He was thinking: Let's get this done. Mom named only the specifics she thought he would need to know at the time. She put some reminders into questions, letting him tell her about the amenities he could remember.

She spoke from her heart, not out of a fear, such as: "Oh my, what if my son leaves wet towels all over the bathroom floor? What if he burps with his mouth wide open? I will be so embarrassed to face Mrs. Smith at the PTA meeting."

She kept the list short and stated rules in a positive way. "I know you will remember to pick up the bathroom when you finish your shower," instead of "Don't leave the bathroom looking like the backyard on a rainy day."

She knew he would make mistakes. There were some things he must learn by trial and error. Feeling a need to reassure Freddie that she cared more about him than the list of rules, she reached out and gave him a big hug. Then she looked him in the eye and said, "I know you will have a great week end with the Smiths. I am confident you will be a good guest."

The Gracious Host

The perfect guest always returns the invitation, if possible. Within a few weeks, Freddie's family arranged to clear their calendar for a free weekend when they could entertain Jason. Freddie wanted to show his friend the same good time he had at Jason's house.

One word comes to mind when we consider what a gracious host does. That word is *anticipate*. Anticipate all the needs your guest might have. For instance, anticipate that your guest will want to know which activities are planned so he will pack the appropriate clothes.

Anticipate the needs of your guests

To begin the teaching, Mom, the sisters, and Freddie might list things they enjoy when they are a guest in a friend's house. Here are some guidelines. Those mentioned in the party section (chap. 13) apply here, also.

- When Freddie's mom extends the invitation, she and Freddie begin their role as hosts. It's important to be clear about the dates and times and any planned activities when giving the invitation, whether by phone, in person, or by mail. Mom will ask if Jason has any special dietary or health needs.
- When Jason arrives, Freddie will take his coat, hang it up, and then show him where to put his things, pointing out where the linens and toiletries are in the bathroom.
- Freddie will introduce him to any family members he does not know. Everyone in Freddie's family will give Jason a warm welcome and tell him to be sure to let them know if he needs anything. They will occasionally ask Jason if he is finding everything he needs.
- Freddie will make room in his closet for Jason to hang his clothes and space in a drawer for Jason to unpack his bag.
- Freddie or his mom or dad will go over their plans for the weekend to see if they are agreeable to Jason.

- Freddie's parents will provide tickets for the amusements for both boys. If Jason insists on paying his own way, Freddie's parents may allow that if they wish. Of course, if Jason's parents picked up Freddie's expenses, his parents will want to reciprocate that favor for Jason. However, when close friends entertain each other often, they usually pay their own way.
- It is always polite to let the guest be first in the activities and to choose the games.
- When the weekend visit ends, Freddie will help Jason gather his things. He will offer him a paper or plastic bag to put his dirty clothes in for the trip home.
- After Jason's visit he will likely write a thank-you note to Freddie's mom. He will thank Freddie again the next time he sees him. When the thank-you note arrives, Freddie or his mom must remember to tell Jason's mom that the note came.

Returning to our word, *anticipate,* we see that being the perfect guest and the gracious host require simple thoughtfulness. To train our children, we show them how to anticipate every need the guest might have by asking them to put themselves in the guest's place. Have your children pretend they are guests in their own house. They will pretend they don't know where things are kept and how things work. Perhaps the bathroom door has an unusual lock, or the shower faucets are difficult to turn unless you know the secret. Make an "anticipated needs list" so you can make your guest comfortable and feel at home.

The perfect guest stays "in favor with men" by promptly writing a thank-you note (also called a bread and butter note) after the visit. The next section will detail how to write such a note and other handwritten hugs.

8

. . .

Mailing a Handwritten Hug

One of the deepest longings in the human soul

is to be appreciated.

Did you ever receive a smudged, wrinkled treasure that your child made for you? A warm hug wraps your heart. You place the prizewinning piece of art on the refrigerator for all the world to see. A scribbled response note or one with a crudely drawn picture grabs your attention and your affection.

"After Christmas my grandchildren always come over to thank me in person," one grandmother told a friend triumphantly.

"How wonderful!" the friend exclaimed. "How do you manage that?"

"Oh, it's easy. I just don't sign their gift checks," replied the proud grandmother.

What happened to the all-but-lost art of writing notes? Perhaps the fun quotient scored low and procrastination won the game. Mom shoves a piece of blank paper under Tony's nose and says, "Write a thank-you note to Aunt Aretha for the amber, anatomically correct antelope ear muffs she knitted for your animal awareness assignment. You cannot play outside until you do." Who would feel thankful enough to write anything after that angry ultimatum? Why not turn the chore into play with a purpose? The promptly written note is the easiest and the most heartily received.

Teaching Your Children the Art of Sending a Note

Create for Fun

By the time children can scribble or make a hand print, they love making things—even notes, birthday greetings, and hand-painted hugs for all occasions. I know; I have some my four-month-old granddaughter made—with a little help from her mom, of course.

By age three or four, Mike can draw a picture of the red fire truck that Grandma gave him. Mom can write beside his picture: "Mike loves to play with the truck. He extends the ladder and blows the siren. He wants to say thank-you." Mike then signs the note with a scribbled name or an "X." By age five or six, Mike can do more. Mom writes the note. Mike prints his name.

A coloring book makes a good resource for finding a picture to trace for a train, a bike, a beach ball, a snorkel set, roller blades —almost any gift. Remember, the artistic correctness is not important unless the child feels that it is. Tracing the picture creates a nearly perfect picture for a little Perfecter. Even a toddler can color a thank-you picture that mom traces. Little fingers eagerly grasp jumbo crayons.

To avoid a disagreeable confrontation, begin training early with fun activities. Let's examine the elements of writing notes: *when to write, what to use, where to write, what to say, how to send them,* and at *what age* parents should begin training their children to write handwritten hugs. Writing notes can be fun. The positive reinforcements our children receive and the appreciative comments they hear will keep the handwritten hugs in the mail.

Answer Promptly

It is always proper to write thank-you notes for gifts or treats within one week. We should answer an invitation within twenty-four hours, but in this age of facsimile transmissions, electronic mail, and families with overworked parents, we sometimes forget to say thank you, much less write it. The written thank-you note seems to have gone the way of the pony express; therefore, we long remember people who take the time and effort to respond in writing to a gift, a favor, or a nice gesture.

Respond to the Occasion

Notes must be written after receiving any gift—birthday, Christmas, graduation, or "just because" gifts. There are get-well notes, "bread-and-butter" notes written to the hostess after an overnight visit, friendship cards, invitations, responses to invitations, and greeting cards. Other occasions for writing notes include (but are not limited to): following a special treat, a trip, or an outing; to a school teacher or church teacher for being a thoughtful, caring teacher; to the custodian for keeping the school clean, etc. Notes are appropriate any time a hug is needed or recognition is due.

Select Pens, Crayons, or Other Tools

Colorful and decorative instruments spark the desire of a young child. Inexpensive supplies are readily available. A "grown-up" ink pen inspires some children. (Used with close supervision, of course.) Give children choices. Let them shop with you for just the right supplies.

Crayons, craft paper, plain white paper, colored construction paper, a brown grocery bag, even leftover wallpaper scraps are among creative choices. Ruled paper is easier for a child to use.

The most popular purchase is foldover paper that measures about 3½" x 5" after it is folded. You may begin writing at the top of the opened notepaper or beneath the crease in the fold. Beneath the crease is preferred. Fold over notes that do not have "Thank you" on the front have long been considered more tasteful.

If your child is a computer enthusiast, let him or her create something on the computer. A gentle reminder: Notes should be handwritten. If you use a printed or computer note, you should personalize it with a few words inscribed by hand.

Find a Place to Write

A small desk or the kitchen table is a perfect place to write a note. Organize the supplies and make them accessible. Procrastination rears its ugly head when we have to rummage around for all the necessary items such as pen, paper, envelopes, and stamps. A small box—plain or decorated—will do. A lap desk with a compartment inside is handy.

Write It with Hugs

"I never know what to say," or "I do not know how to begin." These are common complaints and excuses for not writing notes. Below are some sample notes that you can adapt to fit any occasion.

For the very young writer, saying thank-you for the earmuffs is enough, but as children increase their vocabulary and attention span, more words are in order. Example: "The antelope earmuffs you knitted really made a hit with my teacher and classmates when we presented our science projects on animal-awareness day. You helped me make an A, and I had fun doing it. Thank-you. Your nephew, Bobby."

Mention the Purchase. Sarah writes: "Your check came yesterday. I am saving up for new roller blades. With your gift I can speed around sooner. Thank you very much." We should always state what we plan to do with the money.

Show Gratitude. Letters and notes should talk for us. When we name the specifics, we tell the giver, the host, or the hostess that we mean it when we say thanks. A posted note, no matter the name, no matter the form, warms the heart just the same.

The notes with which we are most familiar are the thank-you note, the invitation, and the R.S.V.P. which is French for "Answer, please."

The "bread and butter note" is one we write to say thank you for the hospitality. An overnight visit or a weekend stay in a friend's home requires a written thank-you note, unless the friends exchange visits often. Very young children can write: "Thank you for inviting me to spend the night. I had a lot of fun."

The older child can write: "What a treat! Thank you for inviting me to spend the weekend at your house. I really enjoyed the games we played and the videos we watched."

Learn the Fundamental Components of a Note.

- *The salutation:* "Dear Aunt Aretha," followed by a comma, is placed about one-half inch from the left margin on small notepaper. (A colon follows the salutation in most business letters.) The writer skips one line, indents for paragraphs, and writes the message, using correct punctuation.
- *The body* of the note contains the message.

- *The closing* belongs on the line below the message toward the right margin. The choice of words implies the relationship of the writer to the giver: "Your loving nephew" is proper. Use "Sincerely" for someone less bonded to the giver.

    Capitalize only the first letter. Two examples are "Yours truly" and "With love." Follow the closing with a comma.

- *The signature* goes beneath the closing. Many errors are committed on this line. Unless the writer is sure the recipient will know which Susie is sending the note, he or she should always sign first and last names without titles such as Miss or Mr. Aunt Aretha will know which one of her nephews received her handknitted antelope earmuffs. Who could forget? Joey may sign only his first name.

- *The date* may be written near the top right margin or at the bottom left margin. The month usually is spelled out: September 3, 1999, or 3 September 1999.

The Thank-You Note for a Birthday Gift

> *Dear Beth,*
>
> *You really know what I like. The latest video completes my set of that series.*
> *Thank you for such a perfect birthday gift. You are a good friend.*
>
> *Affectionately,*
> *Jamie*
>
> *4 October 1999*

The Bread and Butter Note

(Note to the Hostess after an overnight visit*)

> *Dear Mr. and Mrs. Oberville,*
>
> *The weekend at your ranch was terrific. The high point for me was riding the new pony, Sandy. He gave me quite a thrill.*
> *Thank you for inviting me. I had a great time.*
>
> > *Sincerely,*
> > *Joey*
>
> *5 June 1999*

*The old rule had us writing to only the hostess. Today we may write to both host and hostess.

The Invitation

> *Dear Daniel,*
>
> *Please come to my birthday party Saturday, July 20. We will meet at Jiminez Pizza Parlor on Evergreen Street at 6:00 p.m. From there we will go next door to play miniature golf.*
> *My parents are treating my friends and me. Hope to see you there.*
>
> > *Your friend,*
> > *Stan Martin*
>
> *R.S.V.P. 555-4040*

The minimum information includes the *time, place, date,* and *the planned activity.* The invitation implies that Stan's parents are paying for the food and fun.

The R.S.V.P. "R.S.V.P." with a phone number means that Daniel must call. If he can come, he calls to say, "I'll be there." If he cannot come, he must call to say, "Thank-you for inviting me, but I will be unable to come. Our family will be traveling out of state to visit my grandmother. I hope you have a great party. Sorry I have to miss it."

R.S.V.P. stands for Répondez, s'il vous plaît in French.
It means "answer, if you please."

When the invitation has "R.S.V.P." with no telephone number, the answer must be written and mailed whether the reply is yes or no. "R.S.V.P. regrets only" means just that, "Answer only if you cannot attend."

Send It Properly

Janie's mom or dad addresses the envelope. Janie drops it into a mailbox. That gives her a sense of achievement; she knows she has done it the grown-up way. Hand delivery is another option. What's not to love about a special grandchild appearing at the door with a note to thank Grandpa for the gym pass to his athletic club?

Address the Envelope
Block style:

> *Little Miss Beth Allgood*
> *401 Elm Drive*
> *Anytown, Any State 00005*

Indented style:

> *Little Miss Beth Allgood*
> *401 Elm Drive*
> *Anytown, Any State 00005*

Each line of an address on the envelope for social correspondence is usually indented, but the block style is now acceptable. The return address goes on the back flap of the envelope for social correspondence if the envelope is small. For business letters we put the return address in the upper left corner of the envelope.

Note writing is making a comeback. High-level business executives write notes every day. The nature of proper etiquette precludes us from self-aggrandizement, but the truth is that writing appropriate notes is the best public relations we can do for ourselves and our children. People appreciate it when we take the time and especially the effort to send them a note in the mail.

The more notes we write the easier the task becomes. The children I know who are trained early in note writing continue to write them into adulthood. It becomes standard practice for them.

You may know all about writing notes and you may write them regularly. If not, perhaps, some of the suggestions and tips in this chapter will encourage you and your family to begin a life-long habit.

Remember These Points:
- Answer an invitation within days of receipt (within twenty-four hours, if possible).
- Write a thank-you note within one week. (It's never too late.)
- Write the way you would speak to the person.
- Do not mention any dislike of the gift.
- When acknowledging a gift of money, mention what you plan to do with the money.

Try Out These Suggested Activities:
- Write a note to your child, stamp it, and put it in the mail. The message may be a thank-you, an expression

of love to him or her just for being your child. Include a Bible verse. Children delight in getting mail addressed them.

- Let your child see you write notes of all kinds.
- Take your child to a nice stationery store to get a feel for the wide variety of writing instruments and paper. Show him or her the Crane paper, made of cotton fiber, which is the finest quality paper.
- As a goal to anticipate, offer your child a small, personalized supply of stationery when he or she reaches the right age or becomes a frequent note writer.
- As a part of normal conversation, tell Dad in front of the children that you wrote a note to Joe to thank him for his help in repairing the fence.
- Show your child a note you wrote to Mrs. Starnes to thank her for a special favor.
- With your child, write a note to his or her church teachers. Don't forget the department director.
- Write a note of encouragement to a friend or one of congratulations. The best notes of all may be the unexpected.

What better way to "be in favor with God and men" than sending handwritten hugs? In this section we have looked at interpersonal skills that include mouth manners, showing respect, taking responsibility, meeting and introducing, using the telephone politely, being the perfect guest and gracious host, and finally sending handwritten hugs. Mastering these people skills must surely please God.

PART III

· · ·

McTable Manners

The world was my oyster
but I used the wrong fork.

Oscar Wilde

In this section you will find detailed methods to help you teach the necessary dining skills for family-style meals, formal dining, and gourmet restaurants.

Two good reasons to teach dining etiquette to our children: (1) to make eating a pleasant experience for others, and (2) to give us the most practical and logical way to handle our food.

No one should ever call attention to another's dining etiquette (except a loving parent in a home setting). Because of that, no one can correct us. Unless we train our children, they will go through life in ignorance—a great destroyer of confidence. I have adults in my classes who do many things properly, but because they have had no formal training in etiquette, they are ill at ease, wondering if they are doing something wrong.

Our objective is not to turn our children into snobs, puffing them up with pride. The goal is to instill confidence. Confidence in our social skills enables us to focus on others and overlook their faux pas.

9

• • •

Dinner's Ready

*Better a dry crust with peace and quiet
than a house full of feasting, with strife.*

Proverbs 17:1, NIV

Bright, beautiful children turn into ravenous animals when mealtime arrives. Some children clutch their silverware as though they had to hunt and kill the food before eating it. They use anything in sight besides a napkin to swipe their mouths. Chewing with yawn-sized mouths, they grab for food, belch, yell, and hold down the table with their elbows as if it were going some place. If the mood strikes, they exit their chair and wander away, returning at will to mop up what is left on their messy plate.

Our first response is one of near panic: grab the rule books and shovel feed them to all children. But parents who lose are the ones who stress out and become so strict with the etiquette rules that they turn mealtime into a straitjacket experience and rudely teach table manners.

On the other hand, parents who take a too-casual approach to teaching dining skills raise children who think their mud pie table manners are acceptable. Untrained children embarrass themselves terribly out of ignorance when they share a meal with civilized people.

A high school athlete in one of my classes told me the most embarrassing experience of his life was after he was selected athlete of the year. "Why were you embarrassed?" I asked. At a banquet in his honor he ate none of his food. He drank his water and even then was afraid he would make such a serious foul they would bench him for the remainder of the feast.

Perhaps his parents never had an opportunity to learn, and therefore could not teach him. Lack of knowledge is not a character flaw—just a most embarrassing one.

Learning family meal manners is a work in progress. Parents should teach subtly on a daily basis, instructing and modeling good manners. We are all on view. Fair or not, what others see is what they think we are—refined or coarse.

Teaching Family Meal Rules

The easiest way to teach is to turn the dinner table into a battleground with weapons as near as the place setting. A better way is to assume the role of coach. In practice sessions a coach equips and encourages even when offering a critique. The coach instructs in preparation for the game when the player must execute the plays. A coach says, "Watch! This is the way to do it. Let's see you try it."

In a young child's mind the game is just to get food in his mouth any way he can so he can move on to something else. After all, he has to take care of hunger several times a day. "Why should it be such a big deal?" he asks.

Parents wonder how much they should expect from their children. Although what is sufficient for one family may differ from another, some rules should apply to all. Parents also wonder how strictly they should enforce the rules of dining. In our homes we want to feel relaxed and comfortable. We use everyday dishes and paper napkins and coffee mugs. With guests we go to a little extra trouble, not to put on airs, but to show that we care enough to expend the extra effort.

Most children complain about strict parents, but they want rules because they feel more secure knowing their parents care enough to teach them. Most children need an incentive, a reason, for doing anything.

Some Methods

Ideally, Mom and Dad teach in concert. They discuss privately how much to teach and how to do it. Making Mom the ogre is unfair. Also, if Mom corrects Dad in front of the children, she shows very poor manners and sets a bad example.

Here are two suggestions you can use whether yours is a two-parent or a single-parent home:

1. Write some rules on 3" x 5" cards. Let a Powerful or Perfecter choose a card each week before a meal. You may prefer to have the children take turns. Demonstrate the task and then let him or her show the family. Powerfuls like to be in charge, and Perfecters like rules they can check off a list as they learn them. Teaching gives Perfecters the practice they need to hone their skills. The Pleaser likes to follow the leader and will usually go along with the group.

2. Some families enjoy humor and comedy by donning bibs and role-playing. Children see how awful Mom and Dad look when eating with food dripping from

their mouths or reaching for something across the table or grabbing the last piece of roast beef. Try putting mirrors on the table for viewing distasteful habits. The Phun-Lover will love this idea, perhaps too much.

Now, to the genteel, serious parent the comedy idea sounds ridiculous. Different approaches suit different temperaments. Families have temperaments, too.

Another method makes good use of television. Point out the bad manners you see with your child, especially in television commercials. Caution: Making sport of the eating habits of people we know personally shows worse manners than breaking any rule.

"O' would that we could see ourselves as others see us."

ROBERT BURNS FROM "TO A LOUSE"

Embarrassment: An Incentive to Learn

The family dinner table is one of the few warm places left that we can go in our high-tech surroundings. Ideally, the family sits together for a relaxed, pleasant dinner after going in different directions all day. "There is no way," you say?

All of us like to think of our family as ideal, but with work schedules, meetings, practices, games, lessons, and classes, not many of us today have the luxury of sitting down daily to a family dinner—even occasionally might be stretching it. My family found that Sundays at noon after church was our only time together after the boys were old enough to play sports.

The ideal way to practice family dining is daily, but you may have to stage meals for lessons. Why go to all the trouble? Your children will no doubt be the guests of a family or group who eat together. You say there is no one you know who eats that way these days? From experience I can say it is the only way children can be prepared for what could turn out to be some very embarrassing moments. When they become teens or, for sure, when they leave the nest and embark on a career, they will face a test of table etiquette. We all do.

A lawyer I know went to Yale law school and was brilliant enough to clerk for the United States Supreme Court. Each summer the justices include their clerks in a formal farewell dinner complete with finger bowls. You guessed it: the young lawyer lifted the bowl to his lips. Taking a sip he looked around and saw the others dipping their index fingers into the warm, scented water. His crimson face shone. He suddenly felt faint.

Our children may escape such an austere test of table etiquette, but a test will come. That story will inspire some to learn the rules to avoid such a catastrophe. Others will vehemently deny they could ever be so naive as to drink finger bowl water.

The warning of future embarrassment or another incentive should encourage cooperation in learning manners. If your children are so eager to learn your rules that you insult them with such motivation, consider yourself fortunate, but rare. The rest of us need help to whet their appetites, such as a reward or a special privilege or a treat to anticipate.

Dining with the Family

In the following pages is a meal plan for teaching family table manners. The meal is not fancy, and there are no guests present.

Set the table early. Later put the food on the table in serving bowls with serving spoons or forks. The salad will be in individual plates or bowls placed on the table to the left of the place setting.

At your family meal, welcome second servings. Talk about the activities of the day—pleasant experiences, that is. No one but Junior wants to hear about the pickled frog in biology.

Everyone will have dessert together and leave the table after everyone finishes. If a family member must leave to meet an important schedule, he or she will ask permission to leave the table.

For a family meal you need (left to right) a napkin, salad fork, dinner fork, dessert fork, dinner plate, dessert spoon, dinner knife, soup spoon, and iced tea spoon. Bread plate and glasses go above the place setting with the water glass always placed inside.

Place settings can vary depending on the food and the order in which you serve it, but the forks go on the left with knives and spoons on the right. To help children remember that, show them that the utensils spelled with four letters go on the left of the plate. The word left also contains four letters. The utensils on the right contain five letters, as does the word right.

A rule of thumb to remember: Always begin eating with the outside utensils and move inward.

Arriving Well-Groomed

The cook sets the table and pours the beverages (family members may help). She places the food on the table with the salad to the left of the forks. When the cook announces that dinner is ready, all the family members will come to the table with their hair combed, hands and face scrubbed, and fingernails clean. You allow no hats or caps, and no bare feet or torsos.

Assembling at the Table

No one will sit until everyone is standing behind his or her chair. Dad will help Mom with her chair, and the boys will help their sister with theirs. In our dreams, perhaps you are thinking. Try it. They might surprise you. If not, they can watch Dad.

Everyone sits erect with both feet on the floor. Once everyone is seated, Dad says the blessing or names the one whose turn it is. Nothing is to be touched until after the blessing.

Dabbing the Napkin

Mom is the hostess. She teaches the family to watch the hostess at any table for signals such as beginnings and endings. Mom places her napkin in her lap to signal the beginning. Family members place their napkins in their laps, not under their chins like a bib, nor in a belt, nor between buttons on a shirt. Napkins are for dabbing the corners of the mouth, not swiping side to side.

Preparing the Iced Tea

If you and your child are drinking iced tea, you may offer him the sugar bowl or a package of artificial sweetener. With packets, demonstrate how to tear the paper and sprinkle the sweetener in the glass. Place the empty paper on the little dish under the glass.

If the sugar bowl is used, show him how to use and replace the dry sugar spoon in and out of the bowl. Use the iced teaspoon with the long handle to stir quietly. Place the wet spoon on the little dish under the glass, or place the tip of the iced teaspoon facedown on the rim of the dinner plate. Never leave a spoon handle protruding upward, waiting to be bumped.

Never put used silverware back on the tablecloth. Tea stains permanently; therefore, the iced teaspoon is the only utensil that we can prop. When inverted and propped on the rim of a plate, it will not drip a stain.

If you have a lemon on the edge of your glass, take it off, and cover it with your left hand to prevent unwelcome squirts.

Then drop the lemon into the glass or place it on the dish beneath the glass or on another plate if you do not like lemon. Never leave anything on the rim of a glass.

Serving the Food Family Style

Each person helps himself to whatever dish is in front of him and passes the dish to his right. That neighboring person serves himself and passes it on to his table mate on his right. Some manners experts teach "passing food to the left." Elizabeth Post (great granddaughter-in-law of Emily) is today's final arbiter of social etiquette, and she says pass food to the right. My logical reason for this is in the appendix, but if Mom learned to "pass to the left," go with that—just be consistent.

Paper napkins and a paper tablecloth or place mats will do nicely. For even less time and effort, you may fill the plates from the stove and take them to the family, but if you do, have something on the table for the family to pass, such as bread and condiments. Family members must learn to watch their table mates to see if anyone needs the mashed potatoes or some other dish that rests near the observer. He or she is responsible for passing whatever they can easily reach.

No one will begin eating until everyone is served. That may be the hardest lesson to teach.

At Thanksgiving you may want to use the most formal style of family dining. Place the dinner plates in a stack in front of Dad. He will carve the turkey, serve a portion onto each plate and pass the plates down the right side of the table stopping with Mom and working back up that side, then down the left side to the person on Mom's right working back up the left side to serve himself last. The other dishes are passed around the table.

Communicating Over Dinner

The socialization of our children begins around the family dining table. Conversation will usually take care of itself. Be sure to draw out the least talkative member by asking questions, such as, "What did you do today, Jimmy?" or "How was your math test, Mary, hard or easy?" It is better to ask "What did you learn today?" than "What grade did you make?"

Exchange comments as if you were playing tennis. The ball goes back and forth. One family I know has a unique way of making sure everyone gets equal talking time. You may want to try it. They place a timer on the table, and a bell signals the time to change speakers.

Passing and Requesting Food

Mom and Dad set the example by watching to see who needs another serving. One of them might say, "Ben, would you like more potatoes?" Ben responds, "Yes, please." The potatoes are nearest to Mary. She passes them to Ben who serves himself and asks if anyone else would like more potatoes. If not, he sets the bowl on the table near him. It makes no difference where Ben and Mary sit in relation to one another. We pass food around the table counterclockwise the first time only.

After that, whoever is nearest the dish passes it the shortest route to the person who needs it.

Each member of the family should be encouraged to ask if he or she may pass the dish of food nearest to him. He or she should position the serving spoons and forks securely on or in the dish before passing it.

Dishing up Dessert

Remove the dinner dishes from the left or right, but be consistent. At a formal meal everything is removed from the right so that the next course may be slipped simultaneously in front of the diner from the left. Always serve food from the left to prevent an accident, such as when a diner reaches for his glass and the hot dish you are serving collides with his hand. Serve beverages from the right because that's where the glasses or cups rest.

After you remove the plates, set the dessert plates in front of each diner. Pass the dessert for everyone to serve themselves. An easier way is for Mom or an older child to exit the table and place the dessert on the plates before serving them.

When Mom is ready for everyone to leave the table, she will lift her used napkin and place it loosely to the left of her place. She will not refold it. Everyone at the table will place theirs the same way, careful to watch the hostess for the timing.

The males will rise first and help the ladies with their chairs, returning them to their place under the table.

Altering the Plan

You may choose to have a mock session some evening after the dishes are cleared. Set the table and go through the steps, instructing as though there were food on the table. That way Junior won't be dying of hunger while you teach.

If there is no father present, the oldest son can do the honors. If he is too young to handle the responsibility, Mom does it all. She explains the different functions and the rules as the family goes through the meal. Another option is to invite a favorite uncle or male family friend.

If the children in your family have designated chores about clearing the table, those assignments may remain in place.

For this special meal, Mom may choose to make it a special treat by suspending the chores for that evening to do it all herself as another incentive for learning and garnering cooperation from the family. Such a gesture reveals Mom's true motive: to teach manners because she loves her family and wants only the best for them.

Her efforts in teaching do not emanate from a selfish desire to have children who make her look good or to do what some book said she should do.

Parents' prayer for their children:
"Now we pray to God that you [my child] do no
wrong; not that we ourselves may appear approved,
but that you may do what is right"

2 CORINTHIANS 13:7

She wants her children to avoid table stumpers and be prepared for those tests of table etiquette that are sure to come. Parents want their children to be "in favor with God and men" at the dining table, too.

10

• • •

Teaching Formal Table Manners

Manners are noises you don't make

when eating soup.

Formal dinners are served in courses with no communal dishes on the table. Because your child may not be interested in learning formal dining skills, I offer some ways to create a felt need. This plan will involve one child. You may teach the plan to more than one child, if you like, but teaching more than two or three will diminish your effectiveness.

- Ask your child for a date.
- Prepare a simple meal for the two of you.
- Serve and go through the meal in order.
- Later, you will prepare another dinner for you, your child, and the other parent—or some honored adult. Your child will get a chance to practice his newly-learned manners.

- After the first lesson, give your child a chance to teach you some of what he or she has learned.

Some incentives:

- Promise to take your child to an elegant, formal restaurant that offers cloth napkins and clean, starched tablecloths.
- Tell of your plans to reward him or her with a memento to preserve the memory.

How can you know when your child is ready for such a formal lesson? Explain your plans including the fancy restaurant and the memento when you ask for the date. If you get a disgruntled no, you may choose to wait until your child's maturation catches up to your desire—or try another incentive. If you handle it properly, your child should be interested at the right time.

The child must learn to sit through a long meal and skillfully use the silverware. Of course, you should wait until the family dining lesson has been mastered.

Teaching one child at a time makes the occasion more intimate, and you will not be correcting him or her in front of others. Also, he can look forward to displaying his new manners to everyone's surprise.

Your child accepts the date (at home first). The adventure begins. Some children show excitement while others show skepticism. It all depends on the child's temperament.

This meal will be formal in the way you dine, not necessarily in the food you serve.

Preparing the Meal

Prepare a dinner of the foods you know he likes. Serve it in courses: soup, salad, sorbet (optional), entrée, and dessert. If he likes cream of chicken soup, let that be your soupe du jour (soup of the day). It is better to offer him soup that is not chunky so he can learn to sip, not slurp. Consommé or bouillon is a good choice if he likes either.

If he is not fond of green leafy vegetables, prepare a very small portion of lettuce arranged in bite-sized pieces for the salad. Garnish it with colorful shavings of carrots or radishes. Be sure to top it with croutons and his favorite salad dressing. (I often add a few sprinkles of an artificial sweetener. Children often prefer sweet food.)

Prepare any easily cut meat that he likes, whether that is chicken ground hamburger or bologna. Remember, this is a practice formal meal.

Prepare mashed potatoes or small boiled potatoes and green beans, broccoli, or other green vegetable. Less is better.

Prepare homemade or packaged rolls. Showing off your culinary skill with fancy food is not your objective. Just make sure he likes the menu. The purpose of the meal is to make learning a fun experience.

Dessert may be ice cream or a piece of cake. For teaching purposes, make it more challenging to eat by preparing a frozen dessert to eat with both fork and spoon.

Set the table with your best dishes. You will need the following: a large service plate (any dinner plate or charger will do), a soup bowl with a small plate under it, a salad plate (or bowl), a bread plate, a dinner plate, a sorbet dish and spoon (you may use any small bowl and spoon placed on a small plate), a dessert plate, a salad fork, a dinner fork, a dinner knife, a butter knife (you may use another dinner knife if you have no butter knives), a soup spoon, an iced teaspoon, and a dessert fork and/or a place spoon (also called coffee spoon or teaspoon, not to be confused with an iced teaspoon, which has a long handle), a water glass and an iced tea glass. If you do not have both dessert and salad forks in your set of silverware, you may use the same kind of fork, but you will need two of them to complete the place setting.

Place the dinner fork on the left next to the plate. To the left of the dinner fork, place the salad fork on the outside. On the right side of the plate, put the dinner knife with the cutting edge facing left toward the center of the plate. The soup spoon, which is more rounded than a regular place spoon, goes to the right of the dinner knife.

Place a beverage glass at the tip of the knife. The glass should be on a small plate or coaster. Directly above the plate, place the dessert fork with the handle pointing to the left. Above the fork place the dessert spoon with the handle pointing to the right. Place the napkin folded in thirds on the service plate. Place the butter knife across the bread plate.

Serving the Four Course Dinner

Announce that dinner is served. Instruct your child, who has dressed for the occasion, to wash his hands, come to the table, and stand behind his chair until you are standing behind yours. Explain that children wait for adults to sit first and men wait for ladies.

Allow your son to pull the chair back for you to enter. As you sit, grasp the sides of the chair and pull it forward as he gently pushes. After he pulls his chair out and slowly sits, you will talk about how to sit properly at the table—not leaning too far forward or slouching. Sitting bolt upright is also improper. Elbows remain off the table while you eat, and, of course, all four chair legs remain in place.

A good story to illustrate the dangers of tilting a chair backward is about the little boy I knew who flipped over and bit through his bottom lip. That little boy learned the painful way to never lean back in his chair.

If you leave the table to go to the bathroom, quietly say, "Excuse me." Don't announce where you are going. Place your napkin to the left of your plate. Replace your chair under the table. It is rude to leave the table unless you have an emergency.

Saying the Blessing

Say grace and place the napkin across your lap. It should unfold into a rectangle as you drape it in your lap with the open edges toward your waist and the fold toward your knees. Remind your child to dab with his napkin before and after drinking from a glass and periodically throughout the meal. Never dip a napkin in the water glass or crumple it into a ball. Place it to the left of your plate when you leave the table. Never put it in your plate. When dining in someone's home, wait for the hostess to put her napkin beside her plate to signal that the meal is finished. In a restaurant, wait until everyone is ready to leave the table before relinquishing your napkin.

Beverages

Iced tea normally is not served at formal meals, but in some areas it is customary. Usually, only water is served, with coffee afterwards.

Course #1: Sipping the Soup

Finally, it is time for the food. Serve the soup from your child's left. Serving food from the left prevents dangerous accidents. If you serve from the right and the diner decides to reach for his glass, you may scald him with hot soup. Remove empty dishes from the right. Serve beverages from the right of the diner.

After you serve your soup and are seated, explain that the soup spoon is on the far right. Picking up the soup spoon, dip away from yourself allowing the bottom of the spoon to cross the back rim of the bowl to catch any drips. Sip (don't slurp) from the side of the spoon. Try not to make noise.

One of my teen students told me a cute rhyme his mother taught him. It helps him remember the rule: as the ship goes out to sea, I dip my soup away from me.

The rounded bowl of a soup spoon is too large to put into your mouth. Learning to maneuver the soup spoon may take several attempts. Be patient. Dining perfectly is not the main idea. Introducing essential table manners and having fun doing it drives your purpose.

Place the soup spoon on the little plate beneath the soup bowl at all times when the spoon is not in your hand. Never leave a spoon handle protruding above a bowl or glass. Why? If you bump a protruding spoon handle accidentally, out flips the spoon.

If you use a shallow soup bowl with a wide rim, called a soup plate, the spoon remains in the bowl. The spoon handle is not protruding upward to cause accidents as it does in a deep bowl or tall glass.

Breaking the Bread

Now place a hot roll on the bread plate. Explain that you pinch off one bite at a time. Butter that bite, or break open the bread and butter each half. You never hold a piece of bread in your open palm smearing the butter over the whole thing, making a drippy mess.

Now, demonstrate the buttering process. Pass the butter dish and show him how to put a dab on his bread plate using the butter knife. Then put a small amount of butter from the bread plate onto one bite-sized piece of bread.

After using the butter knife to butter the bread, place the knife (cutting edge toward you) on the bread plate. If there is no bread plate, there will be no butter knife. Use the dinner knife and place it across the dinner plate with the cutting edge facing the center of the plate.

Explain that when eating bread we do not eat it with our left hand while feeding ourself with our right hand. We use only one hand at a time, unless we are using both hands to butter or cut something. Do not stuff your mouth using both hands alternately. Your child can hold the bread over the dinner plate to butter it if he cannot reach the bread plate.

Course #2: Savoring the Salad

Remove the soup bowl and the little plate from the right and serve his salad from the left. Then serve yours. Show him how to hold his salad fork like a pencil. Pick up a bite of salad with the fork and lift it to your mouth.

Don't stab the lettuce. Use the points of the fork to pick it up quietly. You may scoop the fork under a bite of lettuce and lift it to your mouth if you can. Long ago, there was a rule that diners were never to pierce the lettuce leaves. That is one rule we thankfully buried.

Explain that seasoning the food before tasting it may hurt the cook's feelings. You can now pass the salt and pepper shakers together, never separately. Place them on the table, not in your child's hand.

When not using the salad fork, simply place it on the salad plate, tines turned upward near the center of the plate. Point the handle to the right.

When both of you have finished your salad, remove that course from the right. If you like, you may serve sorbet at your formal dinner.

Served immediately before the main course, sorbet is a frozen mixture of fruit juices. It cleanses the taste buds in anticipation of the entrée. You will find a recipe in the back. Serve it in a small compote dish placed on a paper doily on a small plate. The sorbet dish and plate are placed in the center of the service plate in front of the diner. The sorbet spoon is on the plate holding the sorbet dish. When that course is finished, remove the sorbet dish and the big service plate, leaving an empty place on the table.

Course #3: Serving the Entrée

Serve the main course of meat and vegetables. Place your hands near the knife and fork. Say, "What do you think we will use to eat this course?" Prepare to teach your child the American style of eating or the Continental (European) style, whichever one is customary in your house. The Continental style uses the fork in the left hand to bring food to the mouth after the food has been cut. The American style is to switch the fork to the right hand after laying the knife down. Both ways will be explained in detail in appendix C. Both ways are correct. Just make sure that if you eat Continental style, the fork remains inverted in the left hand. You may not mix the two styles during one course, and you may not hold the fork in your left hand with the tines pointing upward unless you are left-handed.

Wielding the Knife and Fork

Show a right-handed child how to cut his meat by holding his knife in his right hand. He will hold the inverted fork (tines downward) in his left hand. The rounded end of the knife handle will point into the palm of the right hand. The index finger will rest on the dull edge of the knife. For a left-handed diner, reverse the hands. (Some left-handed people are ambidextrous when it comes to dining.)

Demonstrate how to place the fork tines on the meat. Cut one small bite at a time with the knife. You may have to stand over him and help him, but let him try.

Invert the fork in your left hand. Rest your index finger on the spine of the fork handle. Cut the meat with the knife, holding the fork nearer to you than the knife blade. Cut away from yourself. A common mistake is to hold the fork like playing the cello; that is, with fingers gripping the fork handle while sawing with the knife blade across the fork. Also, do not cut between the tines of the fork.

If your child becomes frustrated or bored at this point and wants to get on with the game, you may be trying to teach too many things at once. If two or more children are learning together, they should be of similar maturity levels because dexterity varies with age.

The only failing grade for this project goes to the parent who loses patience or forces the child to continue after the fun ceases. There will be other meals and other opportunities. Be quick to chart and praise the techniques he learns.

If you are unable to complete the meal exactly as you planned, take heart; your preparation and efforts will be worth it. Do not force your child to endure the lesson you worked so hard to prepare. Timely bits of humor will prevent thwarting your efforts. Examples: "You don't have to stab the chicken leg. It's already dead," or when you see him hunched over the table with his arms circling the plate, ask him if he is guarding his plate from possible theft. If he holds his fork like a shovel, you might say, "Is it really that heavy?" If humor is not appropriate, discuss the perks of learning manners. You want to insure your future opportunity to teach.

After cutting a piece of meat, show him how to lay the knife across the top of the plate turning the cutting edge toward the center of the plate. You might want to relate the following reason for the placement of the knife.

Long ago, men waved their razor sharp knives around, gesturing as they talked. They could easily cut their neighbor's nose, so they came up with the following rule: Every man had to turn the sharp edge of his knife toward himself. Today, placing the knife that way shows that the user probably attended a class or learned the proper way at home.

Place the knife properly then shift the fork, holding it with your right hand like a pencil. Gently put the points of the fork into the meat and lift it to your mouth.

Show him how to spear the vegetables gently and quietly, being careful not to put too much into his mouth at once.

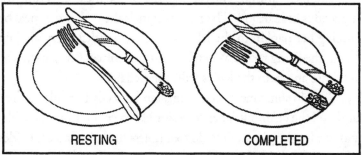

RESTING   COMPLETED

When reaching for your glass, place the fork near the center of the plate with the tines pointing upward. Never "gangplank" it with the handle resting on the table like the oars of a row boat. Remember, the iced teaspoon with the long handle is the only piece you may prop upon something.

When the main course is completed, place the knife (the cutting edge toward the user) and the fork parallel on the plate diagonally from upper left to lower right with the handles pointing to the right. If food remains at the top of your plate, move it toward the center with your fork. The cook now removes the dinner plate and the bread plate. Only the dessert pieces remain at the top.

Course #4: Anchoring the Dessert

Serve the dessert on a dessert plate. The following instruction is for right-handed people. Explain that accidents often happen with frozen desserts. If you cut into a hard dessert, sometimes it flies off the plate and embarrasses the diner. With your fork inverted in the left hand, hold your spoon in your right hand like a pencil, using it to eat the dessert. Right-handed people always place a spoon in their right hand. Left-handed people hold spoons in their left hand. If you have ice cream in a dish, a spoon at the top of the plate is all you need to eat the dessert. If you have an unfrozen piece of pie or cake, you need only a fork.

Concluding the Four-Course Meal

You have finished the dining part of the meal. It is time for a gracious conclusion. The hostess signals the end of the meal by placing her napkin to the left, as she suggests that everyone join her in the living room. When the hostess replaces her napkin, the men rise and help the ladies with their chairs.

To help someone with a chair, stand directly behind the chair and pull the chair out far enough for her to get up from the table. No one is strong enough to do that unless the lady grasps the sides of the chair and helps guide it backward. No matter how big he is or how tiny she is, he cannot move that chair without her help. He returns the empty chair to its place beneath the table.

Celebrating the Manners

Prepare the same dinner for your child, yourself, and the other parent or invited adult. The big test is not for the child, but for the parent who instructed. Why? Because the temptation will be strong to teach and correct and admonish lapses of memory.

Nevertheless, this is your child's moment to shine. Your future opportunities to teach manners and your child's desire to learn are at stake. Reprimanding, correcting, scolding (even gently) will discourage and frustrate him and do more harm than all your hard efforts in didactic.

Correcting without Embarrassing

So, what are you to say when he leaves his spoon handle protruding upward in the glass? Nothing. Just stare at it periodically. He will probably correct his own mistake. Now is the time to let him correct himself, and he will usually do that if you give him a chance. Once he catches his own mistake, he will likely remember to do the proper thing in the future.

That is what you want. You will not be at the fancy dinner when he goes for the big interview with the top executive for his first big job. Your responsibility is to nurture a desire in him to do the correct thing for his own self-confidence. Making people around him feel comfortable boosts good feelings about himself and encourages others to like him. That is what you want to accomplish.

A favorite Sunday School teacher gave me this axiom when I was a young mother: A mother is someone to lean on who makes leaning unnecessary.

Before the celebration meal, have a talk with him. Tell him that you will not be correcting him unless he asks. He can watch your eyes to see if he is making a mistake. That way, he will feel that he is displaying his new manners on his own. Encourage him to ask questions during the meal if he has forgotten a point or a method of doing something. It is imperative that your child is confident that you will never embarrass him.

What about correcting the other parent or adult at the table? No, unless he or she requests the information. The other parent can say to the child, "Now, at this meal, please tell me if I do something improperly."

Always treat your child as you would a guest in your home. If we said to a guest, "Sit up straight, hold your fork correctly, don't talk with your mouth full," that guest would likely never return. Our children deserve the same consideration. They are infinitely more important to us than a guest. We all want our children to do well and to have good manners. Do not let fear for their future, what others think of you as a parent, or time pressures sabotage your efforts. Having a plan will bring long-term benefits.

Reinforcing the Training

Ask your child if he would like to be the teacher. Choose a meal when the two of you will be alone and the child is interested. Let him feel he is in charge.

The meal may not be as elaborate as the formal one. It may not be served in courses. Ask questions such as: "What do I do with my knife after I use it? I know I cannot place it on the tablecloth."

Leave your iced teaspoon in the glass and let your child point that out to you. Let him show you how to butter your roll. The best way to reinforce any learning experience is to try to teach it to someone else.

After reading all this tedious, formal, and didactic exercise, you may wonder why we go to so much trouble to dine formally. Why so many rules? Doesn't it make us pompous pretenders?

Every rule of etiquette has a practical reason. The overriding reason behind all of the rules of etiquette is simply to know what is proper and what is not so we can enjoy the food and the people in a quiet, congenial atmosphere. If we follow the rules, mishaps and offensive behavior won't spoil everyone's meal and embarrass us.

Eating out becomes increasingly more convenient for us. In public places our dining skills or lack of them are on display. Knowing what to do and when to do it relieves our self-consciousness and fear of embarrassment. Then we can focus on the food and fellowship, thus providing more opportunities to be "in favor with God and men."

11

• • •

Dining Out with Babies and Toddlers

A man finds out what is meant by "a spitting image"
when he tries to feed cereal to his infant.

Most of us can remember dining out with our precious baby or toddler and being so embarrassed that we lost our appetite or looked for the nearest exit.

The very thought of dining out with children brings visions of knocked-over glasses, mashed potato and ketchup creations, and screeches of "yuk" at the sight of raw oysters slipping from the half shell down the pallet of the diners at the next table.

We think of children bouncing, squirming, and flailing their arms. Their excited voices jump octaves and decibels. We remember our one-year-old banging the spoon against the highchair. At the "terrible two's" mark he was not any tamer. The ages between one and five are the difficult dining years. Well, we can continue eating carry-out food and risk permanent indigestion or plan a strategy.

131

It is just not reasonable to expect children under the age of five to spend an entire meal at a restaurant without getting restless. Parents and restaurant personnel are understandably nervous. We ask energetic youngsters to remain immobile for what seems a church-service eternity while the grownups dine.

We dare to venture out because we have our own social needs, and we know that taking children out in public helps them develop proper public behavior. We hope to send them out into the world as civilized adults equipped with good table manners.

Yes, dining out with young children can be amusing, exasperating, intimidating, and embarrassing, but with preparation we can minimize the gaffes. One mother told me she takes newspapers to spread under the chair because her child is especially prone to drops and spills. I thought my children were messy, and I never did that. But then, maybe I never thought of it.

How to Dine Out with Young Children

Keep the Temperament in Mind

Why are the children of other parents so well behaved? I am sure you remember seeing the young parents in a restaurant with their angelic newborn. You know, the one whose mother was back to a size six and the proud father was showing off his newborn to all who would gaze.

And there you were with your four-month-old, squealing baby. Take comfort in knowing the fault may not be yours. Your child's temperament, or likely your baby's digestive tract, is a major contributor to his behavior.

That angelic newborn may turn into a Phun-Loving toddler who wanders among neighboring tables like an ambassador of the circus, capturing the crowd's attention with piercing shrieks that could shatter glass. Your comparison of the two children may be only your perception of the situation.

A child's temperament will often determine if he greets everyone he sees with a big smile (Phun-Lovers and Powerfuls) and how long you can expect him to remain contented (Pleasers and Perfecters) before the food arrives. Regardless of the child's natural bent, the prepared parent is a confident parent.

Have a Plan

- Begin the training at home. A few simple goals for toddlers might include: using a napkin, saying please and thank-you, and asking permission before leaving the table.
- Reinforce good behavior with specific praise and your own example of polite table manners. If you eat in a relaxed but controlled way, taking pleasure in each other's company, your child will get a more useful message than he will from a scolding.
- Rehearse at home by roleplaying. Big brother (or Dad) can be the waiter, and big sister (or Mom) can be the waitress. Dressing up can instill pride and the desire to behave well.
- By age five, he may be ready to learn to chew with his mouth closed and use his silverware for eating, not playing tunes on the water glasses. Teaching too much too early can be counterproductive—like potty training. Rushed children sometimes revert to diapers. The finer points such as distinguishing the salad fork from the dessert fork can come later. Watch for success in one area or even occasional success before teaching more.

When you are ready to venture out with your baby/toddler:

- Tell your roving little table hopper (if he is old enough to understand) that he will be expected to remain in his seat at the restaurant. Teaching self-discipline is the goal; therefore, we don't fuss at him for being friendly.

- Choose a time when he or she will not be cranky or sleepy. Arrive early to avoid the peak serving time. Choose a quiet corner or a spacious booth. Select a room with a view, if possible. A window seat will help keep a child amused.
- Familiarize your child with a booster seat placed in one of your dining chairs. You may want to take your own with you. Let him learn to sit for longer periods of time throughout a meal at home to match the time in a restaurant waiting for food.
- For restless little ones, take items such as a bottle or cup with a spout, teething biscuits, or maybe small toys. An older child will enjoy wrapped snacks, crayons, a pad and pencil, or a dot-to-dot or sticker book. Some restaurants provide artistic materials and post the creations on the walls as an ever-changing display.
- Empathize with a two-year-old by telling him, "Look, I know it is hard to sit still, but you will make us all happy if you can do it. We like taking you with us."
- If you think your child may turn up his nose at the food because it is ethnic or too spicy, take along a peanut butter and jelly sandwich, a bagel, or a small package of cookies (if he has eaten his meal at home). Children act out more when they are hungry or sleepy. A back-up snack can forestall a scene.
- Restaurants are not the place to introduce a child to new food. Even a hamburger can be revolting to a child who has unusual culinary tastes.
- Consider the type food you may encounter before you dress your child. Mustard and ketchup do not wash out well. Velveteen dresses and wool trousers are not good choices. An expensive, soiled outfit is a permanent reminder of a difficult dining experience.

Choose the Restaurant

- If you are new to a city, explain the ages of your children and ask for suggestions from friends, relatives, or neighbors. Choose a casual restaurant with paper napkins, not one with a four-star rating.
- Ask if the restaurant furnishes highchairs or booster seats. You may need to take a clip-on seat that fits most table tops. You can always use a large telephone directory.
- Before introducing children to an elegant restaurant, start with a fancy dessert place.
- Ask if baby strollers are permitted. Don't count on it; they block walkways.
- Ask to place your food order ahead of time to avoid a long, hungry wait upon arrival. Babies and toddlers do not wait patiently when they are hungry. Even school-age children squirm after about forty-five minutes.
- Restaurants with all-you-can-eat buffets offer a way to feed the family early with no waiting.
- You may want to choose a restaurant that will take special orders. If your Susie won't eat tomato sauce, she will want her spaghetti served plain.
- A neighborhood place where the waitress brings a cold drink to the table right away and offers a friendly hi to your child can be a dining place you will visit often.
- Choose a restaurant that welcomes children. Forget the fancy decor. Look for the right atmosphere, the right food, and a serving staff that won't see your children in tow and try to serve your family in the kitchen.

If you call a restaurant and learn that children are not welcome, you may resent it, but you will resent it even more if you are turned away at the door.

When Trouble Brews

Some parents ignore all shrieks and every uncouth antic their children perform, to the dismay of all the other diners who must endure the mayhem.

Other parents reading this have none of these problem children and wonder what all the fuss is about. They discipline their children, and they always behave. Then there are parents like you and me. We discipline our children, and they still misbehave, especially in public places.

If we eat out in restaurants the unexpected often occurs. If our child causes a commotion that disturbs other diners, we should be prepared to handle the situation even if it means leaving. It is not fair to the child to make him stay and cruel to the other patrons who are paying their money to enjoy a pleasant meal.

If a battle arises over the menu, parents can keep the peace and teach early decision making by limiting the choices.

If Susie is getting restless, she may not be doing it to be mean. Parents should not embarrass her. They can ask if she would like to walk around or go to the bathroom. Of course, she may be acting out so she can leave the table for any reason.

If children should know better than to blow bubbles in the ketchup with their straw, they should be told once to stop. On a second infraction we need to take them outside or to the rest room immediately for consequences that we have explained earlier.

If a child seriously misbehaves, consider getting a sitter the next time and explain why that child is not going, suggests Katherine Kersey, Ph.D., of Old Dominion University in Norfolk, VA.

Once we convince our children that we will not tolerate their running around, we can usually enjoy a pleasurable and educational experience eating out with the family.

Using some of these tips should make dining out something special—an anticipated goal for a child. If all your best efforts fail, and you have to leave the restaurant, take the food home. There will be better trips eating out and better days to come.

From Our Child's Point of View

As parents, we are on stage performing before our children. How we treat waiters and waitresses is important. Children see us leave a sufficient tip. A tip of 15 percent is the minimum. In elegant, pricey places, 20 percent is the minimum.

Children watch to see how Mom and Dad treat the waiters in trying circumstances, such as when the order for a well-done steak comes floating in red "au jus." The waiter did not cook the meat. We should firmly, but tactfully, ask the waiter to return it to the chef for more grilling. We should discreetly complain to the maître d'hôtel or manager.

If the bill arrives with a math error, one parent should politely say to the waiter, "Could you recheck the numbers on the bill? I don't seem to come up with the same total."

When a child asks, "Wasn't I good?" the parents have neglected a fundamental principle of teaching manners—encouragement. Just as success breeds success, praise and positive comments along the way breed better-behaved children. If we search, we can find some act or omission to praise.

All children like to please. Some thrive on it. Parents should praise according to the child's temperament. Suggestions: To the Powerful: "You were patient and kind this evening;" to the Phun-Lover: "Thank-you for keeping your voice low and not laughing too loudly;" to the Pleaser: "Thank-you for making a quick selection from the menu;" and to the Perfecter: "You remembered all the etiquette rules we discussed at home."

Next, we will learn how to eat on the fast track in fast-food places as well as dine at four-star restaurants.

12

• • •

From Pizza
to Gourmet

The greater the man,

the greater the courtesy.

P laces to eat out include fast-food drive-ins, cafeterias, family-style restaurants, pizzerias, buffets, and four-star restaurants. At a four-star restaurant, the food may not be better, but the decor usually is. Gourmet food is on the menu. Customers dress up more. A maitre d' shows customers to a table with cloth napkins and tablecloths. A head waiter may take the order with waiters or waitresses bringing the food.

Gourmet restaurants may serve a dish of sorbet just before the entrée. Sorbet is frozen fruit juice and cleans your palate before the main course. You do not order it. It comes with the meal. Some restaurants perhaps unwittingly serve sherbet and call it sorbet, but sherbet coats the mouth instead of cleansing it. Sherbet is usually less expensive. Your servers may not realize the difference is important.

Family-style restaurants are not as formal. The silverware is wrapped in a paper napkin. There is no bread plate nor service plate and often no tablecloth.

Buffets usually are places where customers pay one price and eat all they want. Cafeterias are much like buffets, but quieter, less rushed, and they usually offer more choices. Customers or waiters remove the dishes from the tray and place them on the table. Tipping is not necessary unless someone carries your tray or does a favor. Tip a waiter at the time of service. You may not see that person again. He may not clear your table.

No-No's in Any Dining Situation

No-no's include but are not limited to: stacking dishes, blowing through straws, throwing things, dangling a spoon from the nose, making loud noises, being rowdy, playing tunes on the glasses, blowing bubbles, putting gum on or under the table, making noises with food, drink, or straws, building houses with packets of crackers or other condiments, writing on the tablecloth, wasting ketchup by making puddles, crunching ice, writing on walls, pulling tricks on the waiter, making a gooey mess with food, not flushing the toilet in the rest room, throwing paper towels on the floor, leaving the water running in the lavatory.

Caution to parents! You will want to keep this list from all pranksters. I don't want to add to their lists of tricks. They could add to mine, I'm sure.

Bad Manners in Drive-Ups, Salad Bars, and Buffets

Bad manners in fast-food eateries, salad bars, and buffets and pizzerias include: taking too long to order, arguing with a family member about choices, not saying please and thank-you to the one who takes the order, placing complicated special orders if others are waiting in line, taking more napkins, straws, and other supplies than needed, taking packets of condiments home in a pocket, piling a plate too high, searching too long in a dish for just the right tidbit, leaving a messy table, wasting food in an all-you-can-eat place, sharing a plate with someone who did not pay for the all-you-can-eat fare, using one's fingers to take food, returning food to the dish after choosing it. (If you find a spoiled tidbit or morsel on the buffet table, summon a server or put it out of sight. Don't just return it to the dish.)

Dining in a Four-Star Restaurant

A grandmother enrolling her grandson in one of my classes told me about taking him and two of his friends out to eat in a fine restaurant. One of the boys ate everything with his fingers—even the salad. He squashed his food, stacked it, rolled it around on his plate, and stuffed handfuls in his mouth. The other boy used his fork but drowned everything in ketchup and talked with food in his mouth. Food was all over his face, and he never picked up his napkin.

One of the main reasons we have mealtime rules is to make everyone's dining experience gastronomically pleasant. Clearly, these young boys did not plot and plan to be offensive, but in their untutored condition, they did need some training.

You have taught family manners and formal dining manners to your child. Now it is time for the fancy, four-star restaurant. You will know when your child is ready for this experience.

Occasions that call for such a celebration include: a reward after the lesson in formal dining, a birthday, a graduation (of any kind), entertaining a special guest, a Christian confirmation or baptism, a Bar or Bas Mitzvah, a reward for some accomplishment.

If you dine in a restaurant to practice the formal table manners, explain that the personnel may not serve the meal exactly as you did at home. Tell your child that you will quietly explain the differences as they occur.

Arriving at the Restaurant

Wait at the entrance to be seated by the hostess or the maître d'hôtel (sometimes called the captain). In any restaurant, if no one seats you, Dad or the adult in charge leads the way to a table. Ladies sit first while the men help them with their chairs.

A booth seat against the wall is a banquette (ban-'ket). The mother and girls usually wait for the waiter to pull the table out for them to enter. Men and boys sit on chairs opposite them. Make sure your child is seated high enough and close enough. You may need to ask for a booster seat.

When everyone is seated, unroll your silverware and place it in the proper places. Put the napkin in your lap as you did at home. If a fancy napkin is in front of you, the waiter may drape it in your lap. Look around to see if waiters are doing that before reaching for yours.

Crackers, condiments, and water should not be touched until the first course is on the table, which may be salad or soup. You appear ill at ease if you reach immediately for a drink of water or a package of crackers.

Selecting the Food

Ask the waiter to make menu suggestions if you are unsure. Chopped steak is a good choice for a child. Table d'hôte literally means the host's table. For diners it means the complete meal selection is one price. À la carte means that items are priced separately.

Dad or the adult in charge asks the family members their choice of entrée. When the waiter comes to the table, Dad places the orders. Then when the waiter asks, each person names his or her choice of salad dressing and other condiments.

Tasting New Food

Ordering exotic food the child has never seen may present a plate of expensive food that no one can eat. It is fun for each person to order something different to allow new tastes to develop in the family. Messy foods such as spaghetti, lobster, crab legs, or escargot are difficult even for adults to manage.

Now you await your food. Hoping for an uninterrupted meal, you may want to take your child to the rest room. Also, while you wait, you can answer your child's questions, such as why the waiter wears funny clothes. Other good topics are the decor or the history of the establishment, some specific points of formal dining etiquette, or even the reasons behind the rules. Seize opportunities to teach when a child is receptive. Here he is a captive audience, and he knows this is a special treat.

Be sure to make explanations brief, and allow him to talk, too. Answer one question at a time. Give only as much information about a subject as he asks.

Receiving the Food

If the waiter offers to pour a beverage you do not like, simply say, "No thank-you." Nothing (including the waiter's hands) should ever touch the rim of your glass or cup except your mouth; therefore, do not place your hand over it. If the glass or cup is inverted, you may leave it, but don't invert it yourself to show that you refuse the beverage.

After you receive your beverage, you may prepare the iced tea, placing the paper wrappers of the sweetener or sugar somewhere out of the way (an unused ashtray, your bread plate, or the little plate under a glass).

Unfold the foil butter packet. Slide the pat of butter off the foil with your knife and onto the bread plate. With no bread plate, you may place the butter on your dinner plate. To prevent a mess, fold the foil wrapper before placing it on the bread plate or dinner plate, never under the plate.

Never clap your hands, snap your fingers, or call out, "hey you" to attract a waiter or waitress. If your waiter is inattentive and you cannot make eye contact with him, ask another waiter to summon your waiter or waitress.

If someone at your table must send food back for any reason, the others should continue eating slowly while their food remains hot.

Suppose you order an exotic dish, and when it comes you realize you have no idea how to eat it. Ask the waiter or waitress to show you. If he does not know, he should get the maître d'hôtel.

Some friends of ours went out to celebrate their wedding anniversary. They could not read the French menu, so they pointed to something when the waiter took their order. When it came it was escargot, a French delicacy. They did not know they were ordering snails. Not only did they not know how to eat them, they could not even entertain the idea. They should have asked the waiter to explain the terms before they ordered.

What about food sharing? That was once a no-no, but not today—if you do it properly. Perhaps your daughter cannot eat all her meat. Big brother eyes it hungrily. She gives him her plate, and he transfers the meat to his plate with his fork, returning the plate to his sister. Never dangle food from a fork across the table where it could drop.

They didn't know they were ordering snails.

If someone drops a fork to the floor, ask the waiter to bring another one. Do not pick up the fork. If it is in the walkway, you should move it with your foot while waiting for the waiter. You may pick up a dropped napkin, or you may ask for a new one.

If someone spills or drops something, or errs in another way, scolding him or her in public is a serious breech of etiquette. Summon a waiter, excuse yourself and your child, go to the rest room, and repair the damage.

If your child suddenly must return to the bathroom after the food arrives, he should say, excuse me, without announcing his plans. You and your child will place your napkins, clean side up, to the left of your plate or in the chair. When you return, place it in your lap where it will remain until you leave the restaurant. A word of caution: These days a young child should never enter a rest room except in the protection of an adult.

When Someone Stops by to Visit

If a gentleman stops by the table to chat, Dad rises to greet and introduce the friend to the family. He shakes hands. If Dad goes blank on the man's name, he can say, "I would like for you to meet my family." He hopes the visitor will introduce himself. If the group is large, or there are several visitors at one time, it is not necessary for Dad to make introductions. Visitors must not tarry. Food gets cold quickly.

When a man finds it awkward to rise from a seated position, he may place his hands on the table and lift himself slightly to show his manners. If he is in a cramped space, he may remain seated and just nod his head to acknowledge someone.

To discourage long conversations with "happen by" visitors, you should be polite but brief in answering questions posed by the visitor. Don't ask many questions. You hope the visitor will notice your food losing heat by the syllable.

Concluding the Meal

Two items that set a four-star restaurant apart from the others are a dish of sorbet and a finger bowl. (see appendix A) Diners do not order sorbet from the menu. It is a natural part of an elegant meal.

Another distinguishing characteristic of a fine restaurant is a finger bowl delivered after the meal. It may contain aromatic flower petals.

More than one unwary diner has lifted his finger bowl to drink the water. I thought that was a joke until I heard school teachers and other professionals in my classes relate their embarrassing faux pas.

Watch the person in charge at your table for your cue to use the finger bowl. Dip one index finger in the warm water and gently rub the fingers of that hand together and dry them on the napkin in your lap. Then dip the index finger of the other hand. Do not raise the napkin to meet the bowl. Dry your fingers at the table's edge.

Sometimes the waiter will bring the finger bowl on the plate where he will serve the dessert. He will place the bowl (on the dessert plate) on the table before you. Lift the bowl and the doily beneath it. Place them above your place to the left. The dessert plate remains in front of you to hold your dessert when the waiter serves it. Later you will use the finger bowl after the waiter removes your dessert plate.

Sometimes waiters bring finger bowls after a lobster feast. I always wish for one when I eat in a restaurant that serves honey and biscuits, but that is usually served in an informal restaurant. In Chinese restaurants, waiters sometimes offer warm, wet towels.

Paying the Bill

The rules in the informal section apply. Even in an expensive restaurant the payer should discreetly check the math on the bill. Sometimes the restaurant includes the tip in the total. At least 20 percent is customary in many regions. In some parts of the country it is often more. The transaction of paying the bill occurs at the table with the waiter or the captain, whoever brings the bill.

Gentlemen rise to help the ladies with their chairs and their coats if they wore them. If the wraps were checked at the entrance, a gentleman retrieves the lady's coat.

Whether we take our children to a pizzeria or a gourmet restaurant, we can all dine more enjoyably if we prepare and train our children beforehand and along the way.

Happy dining!

PART IV

• • •

Public Behavior for Public Places

Mind your manners so

no one will have to mind your bad manners.

In the *Parade* section of the newspaper recently, Bill Gates of Microsoft, Inc. said that any kid who grows up twenty years from now will be able to go to the library and browse the world's knowledge on computer, be tested on it, and follow it in the direction he or she wants.

Mr. Gates is no doubt correct, but that child will not get the warmth, the passion, the inspiration, or the appreciation for the fine arts from a computer that he or she will get from hearing an Easter cantata in church, a live performance on a theater stage, or a symphony concert. That child will not experience the up-close exhilaration that comes while standing in a museum or art gallery. Teach your children the value of public entertainment along with the guidelines for behaving properly at parties, theaters, concert halls, and churches.

13

. . .

Party Manners

Manners are the happy way of doing things.

Ralph Waldo Emerson

As long as children have birthdays there will be parties. Some will be elaborate and some will be simple. Either way we want our child's birthday to be a happy memory. One of the best ways to celebrate is to plan well, stay within the budget, and prepare the birthday children to be polite guests and gracious hosts. The approach to teaching party manners differs with each temperament. Birthday parties make joyous opportunities for us to get in some manners training. Most children are cooperative because they anticipate the excitement.

Consider the Temperaments

With the Powerfuls—appeal to their leadership qualities. Let them know that this is their chance to be in control—in control of making fun for every guest.

With the Phun-Lovers—appeal to their sensitive, compassionate natures. Tell them that if they are polite and considerate, they will have happy friends. The Phun-Lovers are the most verbal of the four and the most excitable.

With the Pleasers—appeal to their desire to please. They are the least verbal and the most "laid back." They want to please; but we may find ourselves walking them through the greetings at the door, announcing the next game, and taking the initiative. They often appear uninterested. They prefer to be spectators. They make decisions slowly. When planning time comes, they procrastinate. Pleasers show little emotion which perplexes the Phun-Lover parents, unless they accept their Pleasers for the good qualities. Their quiet sense of humor (called dry wit) keeps everyone laughing.

The Perfecters—appeal to their organizational skills. Let them make the lists. They are not as verbal and outgoing as the Powerfuls and Phun-Lovers, but they are observant and very serious. They do things slowly, making sure they do everything correctly. The Perfecters long remember every detail of the party—even more than the parent who is trying so hard to get them excited.

Regardless of the following guidelines, the temperament of the parents and the child will determine the size of the celebration, with the Phun-Lovers choosing the most elaborate.

The manners already detailed in this book will be on display at parties. Specific birthday party manners include age-appropriate planning, invitations, greeting guests at the door, providing entertainment that includes every guest, opening gifts, serving refreshments, and the thank-you's.

The General Guidelines

Go over the party's sequence of events and any reminders with your child before the first guest arrives. After that, take your child aside to clear up any misunderstandings, never embarrassing him or her in front of the guests.

A helper, such as a favorite baby-sitter or an older sibling makes the parent's job easier. Here is a rule of thumb: One adult for every five children under age five, and one adult for every eight older children.

The Age-Appropriate Party

Most experts agree that small parties are the happiest for all, except perhaps for the Phun-Lovers who will make a longer guest list and choose more games. *Good Housekeeping's* Paula M. Siegel says to invite "as many kids as your child's age, plus one."[1] Of course, two guests make a very small party for a one-year-old, but then a party at that age is probably more for the parents than the child.

A family supper for children ages two to three works well or an hour-long party with one or two neighbors or regular visitors.

Four to seven years seems to be the magic age for birthday parties. These children are gregarious. They like entertaining others, as they master the basics of proper manners. Four- to five-year olds love being the focus of attention, getting presents, and participating in games.

The age of the child and the length of the guest list determine how long the party lasts. Before age six, parties usually last one to two hours. After age six, parties may last up to three hours. Children age four to five enjoy theme parties.

By age four the birthday child is ready to help make the plans after the parents set the budget. The child should help make decisions about the guest list, what games to play, the refreshment choices, and when and where the party takes place.

The Invitations

Invitations should be telephoned or mailed about ten days before the party. Be sure to include all necessary information, such as the occasion, the date, the beginning and ending time, directions to the exact location, your child's first and last names, your name if it is different from your child's, your address, your telephone number, and something about the way to dress. The theme or location should determine the attire, which may be casual, dress-up, or costume. Finally, you may include R.S.V.P. with your telephone number, especially if you are paying a fee for each child's entertainment and food.

If parents are welcome, but your budget will not stretch to include paying a fee for all the adults, you may add "food and entertainment prearranged for each child." That also lets parents know the host is paying their child's fee.

The Guest List

- If a guest declines the invitation early, you may invite someone else without mentioning the circumstances.
- Guests and hosts alike should not talk about the upcoming party around people who will not be invited. Age restrictions or limited space may be the reason someone is not invited, but their feelings could be hurt anyway.
- Try to invite at least one person who is a newcomer to your school, church, or neighborhood.

Knowing your children and their temperament blend, you decide how much and how early you choose to expect these courtesies of your child.

If you prefer parties larger in number than your child's age, you may want to consider the following:

- Limit the guest list to the number of friends who can sit around a table. That way all of them can participate and the confusion will not be more than a parent can handle.
- Limit the party time to one and one-half or two and one-half hours.

- Allow about twenty minutes for the guests to arrive and get acquainted.
- Allow about thirty minutes for opening presents or playing games.
- Allow one-half hour to one hour for the entertainment, which may be a magician, a clown act, a movie character, or telling a story.
- Allow thirty to forty-five minutes for serving refreshments, dispensing favors, and preparing the children to leave. The length of the guest list will dictate the length of these approximate times.

The Gracious Host

There are ways to teach being a gracious host, even while we make it a special day for our birthday child. Show him or her things they can do for the guests. Talk about the good feeling we get when we make others happy. To do that, we try to make sure our guests have a good time.

- The focus of the greeting should be joy that the guest has come to the party. Greet the guests at the door and make sure they know everyone. The party child should excuse herself from her guests each time the doorbell rings. She greets the child and the adult, if one comes. She offers to take the guest's coat. She waits for the guest to offer the present before reaching for it. As she accepts it she says thank-you and puts it with the others to be opened later.
- Choose both mental and athletic type games with each child in mind. If a physically disabled child is present, be sure to have some activity in which that child can participate, such as guessing games. The game "I spy" was once very popular. Only one person knows

what the object in the room is, and the others try to guess it. If a child is mentally impaired but not physically disabled, provide at least one game without mental challenges.

- If the birthday child wins a game, the runner-up should get the prize. Before the guests arrive, remind the party child of the rule and explain that he or she will get all the other presents.
- Choose a menu the birthday child likes, but one the other children will enjoy, also. If you are aware of a guest's severe allergic reactions to certain foods, you may try to provide something for that child. You may call the mother to tell her the menu. She may choose to provide alternatives. It is not possible to choose a menu that will fit everyone's tastes. Children on restricted diets usually eat before they come or bring the snack they need.

The Rules for Opening the Gifts

The following rules for opening presents are goals, not mandates. A Perfecter child may achieve them, but a Phun-Lover will forget many of them in the excitement. The Powerful will have a few of his or her own. The Pleaser may say thank-you once, but saying it regularly takes too much enthusiasm.

- Open the gift nearest you first. If you know that someone must leave early, open that present first.
- Before the party, arrange for someone to register each gift and the giver on paper as you open them. Excitement at birthday parties makes it easy to forget who gave which gift.
- Announce the giver and show the present to everyone, or pass it for everyone to see. An exception to that rule

applies when the gift is fragile. A parent may hold it for everyone to see and then place it out of reach.

- After each gift is opened, say "Thank-you, Peter," or "Thank-you, Amy." Add something like, "That is a neat (name the present)."
- If the gift is not one you want for whatever reason, you must at least say thank-you.
- If you already have the item, don't mention it. Just say thank-you.
- Don't say that a particular gift is your favorite.
- Don't comment on how much or how little the gift costs. Relatives often give more expensive gifts than other guests.
- If someone must leave early, leave the gift opening long enough to escort that guest to the door. Again, say "Thank-you for the gift. I am glad you came." (The other gifts will wait for you.)

The Way to Say Thank-You

- Say thank-you if a guest passes a gift to you at the door.
- Say thank-you and name the giver when you open each present.
- Write or telephone the guests later to say thanks again for coming and for the present. If you see the giver often, you may forego the telephone call and express some form of thanks later. If you write a note, you may forego the telephoning and repeating the thank-you later.
- It is never wrong to write a thank-you note, even if Mom or Dad writes it and the child signs it with a scribble. Many etiquette books say that if we thank the person when we open the gift, it is not necessary to write a note. But thank-you notes are always appreciated and often expected. If you are a new resident,

check with someone who knows the local custom for writing notes after birthday parties. Better still, start a tradition. It is great public relations for a newcomer.

The Party Favors

The birthday child will want to give the guests a treat or memento to take home. The favors may be wrapped with the guest's name on it, or they may be passed out as the children prepare to leave. Favors should be alike in size, color, and appeal to avoid conflicts among the children. Theme-related favors made by a parent and the birthday child are always good.

- The birthday child should give out the favors or help mom do it.
- Explain to your child that the favors are his or her gift to the friends who came to the party.

In concluding the party, you may want to read a theme-related book or play a quiet game to calm the children down while they wait for their parents to come for them.

The Gracious Guest

Because "it is more blessed to give than to receive," being a guest at someone's party gives our child a great opportunity to practice good manners. Along with the fun, come some rules of proper behavior.

When the invitation comes, it will name the child who is expected to come to the party. Siblings are not invited unless their name is included. The following guidelines will help parents direct their child in behaving well and being an oft-invited guest.

- Check with your parents and then answer the invitation promptly. Don't say that you will let the inviter know and then forget it.

- If you get permission, say, "Yes, I would love to come to your party."
- If you must refuse, give a reason if you can, such as, "Our family is going out of town that weekend." Tell the truth or say nothing about the reason.
- When arriving at the party, say hello to the parent or parents. Offer your gift to the party child if he or she is at the door. You may give the gift to the adult who greets you, or wait to give it to the birthday child.
- When you are introduced to someone, say hi or hello and repeat the name. Repeating helps us remember.

It is more blessed to give than to receive.

The Present

- Always put your name on a card or on something inside the gift so it won't be lost.
- Don't talk about the cost of the gift you are giving.
- Don't try to get the party child to open your gift immediately or first, even if you must leave early.

The Refreshments

Wait patiently for your serving to arrive. If you see an array of food, don't pick around in it before selecting something. Don't say "yuk" if you don't see anything you like. Take a little, say thank-you, and eat what you can. Don't overload your plate. Later, take seconds only if the hostess offers them. Watch the party child or the hostess for a signal to begin eating the refreshments.

The General Rules

- Be a good sport. Wait your turn. Don't push or shout.
- If you win a prize, say thank-you and don't brag about how good you are. If you lose, don't make excuses or pout.

- Never ask, "When do we eat?" The host or hostess will tell you.
- If you spill or break something, say you are sorry and help clean up the mess, unless the mother says she prefers to take care of it. Tell your mom or dad when you get home so they can offer to repair or replace the object.

The Departure

The invitation will state the ending time of the party. Observe it and say good-bye to the parents and to the party child. If you had a good time, say, "I had a good time." If you did not enjoy the party for whatever reason, just say, "Thank-you for inviting me."

Whether your child is the host or the guest, when the party is over, be sure to give specific praise to your child for the rules your child remembered. Don't expect perfection.

The Swimming Party

"Come any time" does not always mean that you have a standing invitation. In a burst of enthusiasm, pool owners may say this offhandedly as a friendly gesture. Friends should always wait for an invitation that includes date and time to swim in someone's pool.

Swimming pool manners are for fun and safety. Here are some guidelines in talking to your child about swimming manners:

- Be clear about the invitation. Is your family invited or just you and one child?
- Arrive and depart on time. If the hostess sends her children inside to change into dry clothes, or excuses herself, or if the dad comes home, you know it's time to go.
- Be prepared. If you can't wear your swimsuit under your clothes, ask where you may change. Don't leave

your possessions in a heap on the floor. If you must enter the house after a swim, dry off first.

- Bring your own accessories such as towel, lotion, goggles, and life jacket. Make sure you take everything home, so the host family will not have to return something to you.
- Don't intrude on someone's space. If a towel is left to reserve a chair, don't remove it without asking.
- Keep your noise level the same as the host's. (You may disturb the neighbors.)
- Don't drip water on or spray a clothed, dry person.
- Be careful about where you sit in a wet suit. If you are unsure, ask which chairs you may use.
- Don't abuse the lawn. Chlorinated water can kill the grass.
- Eat before you leave home unless you are attending a party with refreshments. Occasionally, take refreshments for everyone, if you are an oft-invited guest.

With caution, even minor accidents can be prevented. Polite, safety-conscious guests get more return invitations. The following rules for safety are helpful.

- Parents must make sure their child will obey the house rules and the adult in charge if the parent is absent.
- Do not run and do not push others in the water.
- Young children who cannot swim must remain at the shallow end of the pool.
- Sharp or metal objects, such as hair paraphernalia, glass, and other breakables, do not belong near a pool.
- Keep the pool area free of chewing gum, food, adhesive tape, paper, and other debris.
- Excessive hair or suntan oil going through the drain can clog the filter.

- Remove dirt or grease from your feet before stepping into the pool. Tiny specks of dirt can mean hours of cleaning for the pool owners after you leave.
- Teach your children never to yell out "help" or "save me" unless they are in physical trouble in the water. Home pools seldom have lifeguards.

Saying thank-you for the swim is a must each time. Writing a thank-you note after the first time is appropriate. After that, a sincere verbal thank-you to the family or hostess, as well as the child, will suffice.

If you do not have a pool and cannot return the invitation to swim, do invite the other child or family for an outing, a party, or some treat in return from time to time.

With the proper training our children can be "in favor with God and men" whether they are cheering at a basketball game or attending the ballet. The next chapter explains the differences in the expected behavior at each.

14

. . .

From Basketball to Ballet

Unruly manners or ill-timed applause

wrong the best speaker or the justest cause.

D id King George II stand during a performance of the "Hallelujah Chorus" from Handel's *Messiah* because he was overcome with exultation, or because he was tired and needed to stretch his royal legs? Most of us prefer the first reason because the familiar masterpiece inspires us the same way— often during the Christmas holidays. Whatever his reason, King George II set a precedent in etiquette that stands today. But he was king. The rest of us must learn the rules of conduct at live performances or risk embarrassment.

When our parents introduce us to the arts at an early age, we can walk with confidence among all social, economic, and ethnic groups. We are forever grateful for those early experiences. Families should be endued with arts education, however limited it may be.

I am not saying that we can expect our children to give up their favorite sports figure for *la ballerine* or *le danseur noble,* but a little exposure to the fine arts is a great learning experience for your child. With the guidelines in this chapter, parents can get some cultural refinement on the family agenda without inflicting culture torture. Mikhail Baryshnikov should be as well known as Michael Jordan. Well, almost as well known.

Athletic Etiquette

Yes, there is such a thing, though we might prefer to call it good fan conduct and good sportsmanship. Most of the rules are for safety. The same good manners of consideration for others apply to all sports events. Guidelines:

- Arrive on time.
- Don't shout insults at the opposing team.
- Stay seated unless everyone stands so that fans behind you can see.
- Take your proper place in line for concessions.
- Don't push and shove when exiting. Walk slowly with the group.

We must teach first by setting a good example at all sporting events. We can teach good sportsmanship at home by playing games, setting an example of tolerance, patience, and cooperation. Sore losers don't make good teachers.

For outdoor public sports like boating and water skiing, your local state department of parks and recreation can provide literature for safety regulations and laws.

Teaching manners at a fine arts performance is a bit more involved than instructing your child not to push and shove at a football game, but the results are worth the effort. Your child will feel confident in knowing how to handle any social or cultural situation.

What Are the Fine Arts?

In a broad sense, the fine arts include music, literature, opera, ballet, painting, sculpture, architecture, and the decorative arts. The word fine means "beautiful" or "aesthetically pleasing." Many great works of literature, art, and music portray religious themes that emanate from artisans of old who were themselves religious. God inspired artists like Milton, Bach, Handel, Michelangelo, Dante, and many others.

How much can parents expect their child to absorb from a performance? Most children prefer doing hard labor to spending time with any form of the fine arts. In this age of visual and musical stimuli overkill, an opera can be a pompous bore to the average youngster. If your child can remain alert for half the performance but sleep through the remainder, he will sustain a modicum of cultural enlightenment, which is far better than none.

Any response you get will probably come in groans and cries of cruel and inhumane treatment. But silently he or she will get memorable exposure to the arts.

Talk about the performers as actors and singers. Explain that the costumes, sets, and lighting help to tell the story. Perhaps most important is how the harmony and counterpoint describe the ways people feel and act. Talk about the pictures that create emotions in our mind, and how they allow us to understand the meaning of an unfolding story.

The title "From Basketball to Ballet" comes from memories of rushing home with our sons from a basketball practice to dress and go to church or a Christian seminar. Occasionally, we squeezed in time for a ballet, play, or concert. Your trek may be from a soccer game to the symphony.

When a young woman takes your adult son to the symphony, he will want to be prepared. Our younger son found himself in just that situation recently. If your son is old enough to be over the "yuks" when he sees a member of the opposite sex, he needs inspiration to get a little culture on his way to manhood.

Attending a Fine Arts Performance

The following are incentives to encourage the child, age-appropriate attendance, the temperaments, arriving and being seated, audience conduct, and what to wear.

Aids to Instill Interest in the Arts

Education about the arts begins at home, and early on, said Jane Komarov, the director of the Met School Membership Program.[1] Children learn best by parental example. (That's a familiar phrase). Ideally, parents together lead the family in arts education, but if one parent is not an aficiendo of the arts, the other parent can manage well.

Choose incentives from the following list that fit your budget and lifestyle.

- Buy or rent a few videos, tapes, or CDs of popular parts of a symphony or opera. The "greatest hits" collection often includes pieces children enjoy. *La Boheme, La Traviata* or *Carmen* are good choices because the music strongly suggests the plot. Your local educational television channel offers a bounty of free performances. Luciano Pavarotti, José Carreras, and Placido Domingo are regulars.
- Listen with your children and explain the story line. Children's books are available to help.
- Begin the attendance phase with productions aimed at children. They may use music, puppets, and child actors. Some performers even ask the audience to participate.
- Experts say the most effective ways to introduce children to the performing arts include: keep it lively and keep it short. Let the children be involved in the

selection, if choices are available. Forty-five minutes to one hour is a good beginning.

- Most cities and some small towns have community theaters and/or children's concerts. Your children may know some of the performers.
- The children's theater is a good place to introduce children to plays, if there is one in your area. Our children loved *Rumpelstilzin*, their first experience at the Little Rock Arts Center. Our two grandchildren recently saw *Three Billy Goats Gruff*.
- Another excellent choice is *The Nutcracker*, which was the first ballet our children enjoyed. With music composed by Tchaikovsky, this ballet enchants children with a Christmas tree that grows and a nutcracker that turns into a prince. A performance is often scheduled in December.
- Live performers present symphonies, concerts, ballets, plays, and dramas. In our technological world of cyberspace, there is something exhilarating about seeing "real" people perform on a stage before us.
- Artistic ability is a gift from God that the performer must work hard for many years to develop.
- Explain to your little sports fan that artistic performers spend years studying, practicing, and training just like famous athletes. Explain that sports have rules and regulations just as there are rules of proper behavior in the arts.
- Parents should not discount school plays, church dramas, and youth concerts. They all require talent and a great deal of discipline and hard work. They are also good places to practice proper behavior.
- Museums, art galleries, and exhibits present convenient opportunities to view great art and historical artifacts.

Age-Appropriate Attendance

The Metropolitan Opera Guild offers a three-part series called "Growing up with Opera," for children six to twelve. Children under school age rarely have the attention span needed for most performances. But just like church services, some children are ready to attend "big" church at age four without disturbing others while we wonder about some at age forty-four. So if the family has tickets to the opera and the youngest child is under school age, evaluate the child and the situation. I would probably get a sitter.

The assistant conductor of the New Haven Symphony Orchestra, Peter Sacco,[2] said a child should not be rushed into a performance hall. He has seen fourth-graders brought who were just not ready for the experience. Again, I say, parents know their children and their ability to remain quiet.

A Look at the Temperaments

The Pleasers and the Perfecters will be the quietest and the most patient of your children. The Pleasers may fall asleep. The Perfecters will remember the details and finer points of the evening. They may even aspire to take lessons in the arts.

The Powerfuls and the Phun-Lovers will be the noisiest. You may have to bargain with them, offering some tangible incentive to solicit their cooperation. By the way, parents do better to bribe than browbeat their children into becoming patrons of the arts or patricians of good manners. Exposure to the arts and good experiences encourage both which ultimately must come from the heart.

Arrivals Suitable for the Arts

Rules or not, what we all want to know is how to attend our first performance without appearing foolish and unschooled in the arts. Oh, the pain of public embarrassment. The arts are not participating sports. They are events to enjoy in silence.

- Strive to be on time, or you may not be seated. Some patrons set their watches ahead to ensure their prompt arrival. Ushers usually lead us to our seats after we give them our ticket designating our reserved place.
- Preceding the males, the females in the family follow directly behind the usher. If there is no usher, the head of the family leads the way down the aisle and waits for the females to enter the row of seats first. Quietly say excuse me to about every third person. Try not to step on their feet. If you enter a row of seats with your back to the stage, you can see the feet to avoid as you make your way down the row. Facing a captive audience also keeps our derriere out of others' faces. You may prefer to face the stage, stepping gingerly without bending at the waist.
- Don't carry purses, bags, and other paraphernalia that are not absolutely necessary to your existence. If you must be a carrier, don't swing your possessions and bump others as you pass. If you do bump someone, say I'm sorry or another polite expression.
- If the performance has started, the usher decides the proper time to seat you. You may have a long wait. People who habitually arrive late to almost everything, seldom arrive late but once to a live performance.
- Don't whisper, rustle paper, rattle, or talk unless you are dying. If you must sneeze or cough, muffle it if you can. If an episode of either one overtakes you, quietly slip out, excusing yourself as you pass.
- Don't hum, fidget, or jangle jewelry, tap with your fingers, open and snap purses, jackets or daytimer notebooks. (Leave the notebook at home.)
- Don't snore. If your partner drops off, you should nudge him or her. It is not bad manners to wake a

snorer unless your partner has a habit of awaking with a start and blabbering unintelligible gibberish.

- Don't express displeasure with groans, sighs, gasps, head movements, or loud laughter. In other words, be as quiet as you would want others to be if you had saved up a year to buy a ticket. Performers appreciate the silence, also.
- See that everyone in your party enters a rest room before entering the auditorium.

Why so many negatives? Knowing what not to do is a major component of good taste. It protects us from offending others. It also keeps us from suffering near-death embarrassment.

Applause. Applause at the performing arts does not get equal opportunity. I will detail the differences.

At the opera we applaud at the end of an aria and after each curtain, but not for the entrance or exit of a performer. At the ballet we applaud at the conclusion of a complete dance or scene. At the symphony we applaud when the conductor or guest soloist walks out onto the stage. Clapping stops when the conductor steps onto the podium and raises his baton. Applause for the music comes only after the conductor turns to face the audience and bows.

The musicians will probably pause periodically. We call these interruptions movements—somewhat like the chapters in a book. Watch for the conductor to turn. That is your cue to applaud.

How to Applaud. Yes, there is a right and wrong way. Clap with the fingers of one hand into the other palm. Clapping palm to palm sounds like slapping. Don't clap your hands in front of your face. Shoulder level is better. Don't clap after others have ceased, no matter how enthusiastic your response.

Attire—Formal or Informal

If you are in doubt about the custom of dress in your area, call the arts center or university and inquire about customary attire for attending the arts concerts in your city.

Patrons usually wear very dressy daytime clothes to an evening performance of the opera, ballet, or theater. For opening night, "black tie" is customary in larger cities. That term means the females wear semi-formal dresses, also called cocktail dresses, and the males wear a tuxedo. If an invitation or billing states "white tie," that means a man wears a white bow tie with a tail coat, and the woman wears a floor-length gown. If you are new in an area, it is wise to ask someone about the local custom. Some areas of the country are more formal than others. You do not want to stand out in the crowd.

Appropriate Manners with Rude People

- First we must remember that some people have never had the opportunity to learn simple social skills. Though we think the rules are just common sense, we must realize that some offenders do not mean to misbehave. They often change their conduct when they redden with embarrassment.
- If someone nearby disturbs you, say, "I am sorry, but I can't hear the performance." Returning rude for rude usually elicits more of the same. If the noise continues, you may ask an usher to call the manager. The alternative is to move to another available seat.
- One etiquette authority says staring "more-in-pity-than-in anger" at the perpetrator is often the most effective way.
- If someone is seated in your assigned place, check your ticket stub and quietly say, "I believe you are sitting in our seats." If the intruder refuses to move, or if you have trouble finding unoccupied seats, return to the usher for assistance. Other members of your party should wait at the back of the auditorium until you have secured seating space.

A Word about Movie Theaters

Once the movie theater was an inner sanctum where we could escape reality by the light of the silver screen. We wrapped ourselves in red velvet darkness enthralled with romantic idealism.

Some modern movie goers are a different breed. Otherwise normal and civilized people seem to change stripes when they enter a movie theater. They confuse theaters with rumpus rooms, and their actions never seem to embarrass them. They slurp, crunch, chomp, crinkle paper, and stretch like tomcats, blocking the view for rows behind them. They talk back to the screen and yak away to their friends in whispers that echo off the walls. They topple cold drink cups that ooze sticky murk into some poor fellow's shoes.

If you have been in one of America's movie theaters recently you no doubt agree that tact and courtesy among movie goers have gasped their final breaths. The president of the National Association of Theater Owners, William Kartozian, says he hears more complaints from movie goers about noisy patrons than any other issue.[3]

All of the above infractions of the Golden Rule cry out for mercy. Parents reading this book have children who may never commit these crimes against old-fashioned kindness and consideration. Somehow, we must get help for the others. Perhaps our children can lead by example.

The best places to learn what it means to be in favor with God and man are the home and a house of worship. In the home, family devotions where God's Word is read daily instills life-sustaining truths about kindness and consideration in our children that they might never get some other place.

Hearing the exegesis of the Scripture from the pulpit and participating in Sunday School week after week will surely help our children grow spiritually and encourage them to practice the rules of polite behavior.

15

. . .

Conduct in Church

Etiquette is what you are doing and saying

when people are looking and listening.

What you are thinking is your business.

Thinking is not etiquette.

Hallelujah, thine be the glory.

Essay from ten-year-old Virginia Hudson,
1904 Episcopal boarding school

Two little boys on the school playground were discussing their idea of church one day. One of the boys said, "When you are little they carry you in on a pillow. In some churches they sprinkle water on your head. When you are older you get dressed up in tight shoes and walk in by yourself.

"The Bible says that you are suppose to grow in your wisdom teeth, build a statue and flavor God with a man. [His interpretation of Luke 2:52.] Finally when you are old you get taken to church again because you are dead. Oh, yeah. In between you go to church to get married. If you are a girl you wear white, and if you spill something on yourself a little girl drops flowers out of a basket on you."

This young child's view of church may resemble the first impression of some adults. Church services are different from most other public gatherings, and unless we grew up attending regularly, we may have little experience with church protocol and the rituals of worship. Whether we are newcomers to worshiping God or have a lifelong commitment and communion with Him through His Son, we want to raise our children to have values and morals in keeping with our country's founding purpose.

The information in this book is, for the most part, directed toward being in favor with man. To do that I feel we must start with being in favor with God. Only He can take our selfish desires and turn them into doing unto others what we like them to do for us.

God does not reside in the church building. He is present with us in every aspect of our lives, but most of us find that a church service and its activities give us the best avenue to show our devotion and reverence to Him.

Jason and Freddie's Continuing Story

Remember Jason and Freddie, the boys who exchanged overnight visits? They became good buddies, which led to the parents of the boys becoming friends. Freddie's parents invited the Frazier family to their church and the Fraziers accepted. Jason's older brother talked often about the Fellowship of Christian Athletes he joined with his track teammates, and the Fraziers had been thinking about finding a church for their family.

Jason's mom and dad went to church occasionally when they were growing up, but never got around to going as a family. The company Jason's dad worked for relocated them frequently, so they seldom put down roots.

Jason's mom knew that she had taught him good manners, and he was well behaved in public, but she wondered how he would do in a reverent church service with protocol Jason had never seen. Track meets and basketball games were their only experience with public decorum. She remembered that the demeanor in a house of worship differed a great deal from behavior in a noisy gymnasium. She decided to explain those differences to Jason so he would be prepared. She wanted his first church service experience to be a pleasant one. They had talked about God, the Creator, so religion was not a new concept to him, just church services.

Jason was a good listener, so all she had to do was find a few minutes when he was not engrossed in his own activities. She compared a basketball game to a church service—sort of.

"At sports events we cheer, jump up and down, eat popcorn and hot dogs, and vent a lot of emotions. At church services we participate by meditating quietly and reverently," she said.

"What's medit . . . and rev . . . whatchamacallit, Mom?" Jason interjected.

"'Meditating' is thinking and 'reverently' is doing everything quietly and at the right time." His mom explained that in church we listen to the music and hear the words of the preacher so that we can think about God and all the good things He does for us. We call those good things, blessings. A verse from her childhood came to mind and she told Jason "every good . . . and perfect gift is from above" (James 1:17).

She explained to him that "reverently" meant everyone bowed their heads and someone would speak aloud to God for all of them in the service. That was prayer. Sometimes there would be no sound at all except perhaps music. That would be the time when worshipers could bow their heads and talk to God by themselves. That was called silent prayer.

She went over some rules about proper conduct in a church and told him that if he just watched her he would know what to do. (Since Freddie's family attended a different church from the one she grew up in, Jason's mom planned to watch Freddie's family closely.) Jason's mom assured him that if he made a mistake no one would notice. A good thing about church was that people accept you the way you are and never yell at you like they do in a ball game. Church services don't have referees because everyone is on their best behavior in God's house.

Seeing a worried look on Jason's face, his mom told him about something she did the first time she went to church. Her mother told her that since she couldn't read music it would be better if she didn't try to sing. Well, Jason's mom liked to sing, and when the congregation stopped singing, and the instruments fell silent, she didn't notice soon enough and out burst her voice in all that silence. She was so embarrassed, but no one got upset.

The next Sunday Jason's mom handed him the Bible she used when she was a little girl, and the Frazier family headed out to meet Freddie's family at church. The Fraziers made some soon-to-be new friends, and they felt like a welcome part of the community. Jason wanted to go back the next Sunday to hear the end of the story the teacher told in the school-like class that he and Freddie went to before the church service.

In the following pages are some guidelines and hints on the P's and Q's of church etiquette and how to get our families to church regularly without losing sight of the reason we are going.

The Sunday Morning Rush

"Hurry, hurry. We are late."

"Don't pester your sister."

"Get your Sunday School (or prayer) book. Well, if you would put it away when you get home from church you would know where it is."

"Change your socks. They don't match."

"Honey, where is my favorite tie?"

"Mom, I had the hair dryer first."

"It is my turn in the bathroom."

"All right. Everyone in the car—right now!"

"Honey, did you remember to set the oven timer? No? Oh, dear. Now, Sunday dinner will be late again."

The Way to Keep Your Religion on Sunday Morning

- Lay out clothes the night before with shoes polished and hair ribbons pressed. (Some parents make a bargain with their child to choose clothes and get approval the night before or wear whatever the parent selects.)
- Get the family up a little earlier. Serve a breakfast that goes down quickly and sticks until noon. (Recipe at the end of the chapter.)
- Don't try to leave a spotless house. After your children are grown, you will have plenty of time for that.

The Parent, the Child, and the Worship Wiggles

- Take a break between sessions. Stop by the bathroom and the water fountain.
- Find a good place to sit. Some children do better near the front where they can see and hear the choir and speaker. Others do better in the balcony. If your child is disposed to frequent rest room trips, sit near a back exit.
- Share the hymnal with your child. Teach him the songs. Most children like to pretend they are reading even when they can't. Teach your child to stand or kneel with the congregation. Some parents choose to allow their child to sit and write or color during these times. The parent can decide how much to expect from each child based on the age and the temperament.
- Try not to compare your child to a well-behaved child. But do consider the adults around you who are trying to worship.
- Praise your child after the service. Emphasize the

behavior that pleased you—"You stood quietly during that long prayer. I had trouble keeping still, too."

- Go to the church's social functions. Children learn how to worship in "big church." They also need to know that church is the place to form lasting friendships with people.

- Remember that your child will make mistakes. One or even several errors will not be the end of the world. Perhaps, you and your child just happen to sit behind a lady with a huge peacock feather protruding from her head. Every time it waves in a burst of air-conditioned breeze, your child laughs aloud and reaches to grab it. Quietly excusing yourself, you may have to take your child out to squelch the giggles. Gently explain the reasons we ignore waving plumes and why we ourselves don't wear them.

- Remind yourself often that most adults around you have been through similar experiences of helping a child overcome the worship wiggles. Most adults believe that nurturing the children in the church is the responsibility of the entire church.

The P's and Q's of Church Etiquette

Question: In what state is it against the law to eat peanuts in church? Answer: Massachusetts

---

Protocol

Protocol in a friend's church may be different from yours.

If friends of another faith invite you and your family to attend church with them, ask about proper dress for men and women. Ask about customs, such as who takes communion and the age children may go to the services and not to the nursery.

Men in Christian churches never wear hats. In orthodox synagogues males always do, and yarmulkes are usually provided for male visitors who arrive without a hat. In many Catholic churches females cover their heads.

Ask what you should take for your nursery-age child. Provide the teacher with any special instructions for your child about feedings and naps. Don't expect the nursery workers to follow your child's routine as though he or she were the only child in the nursery.

Protocol in church greetings require a nod and a smile, and perhaps the exchanging of names. Discussions should take place outside or in the foyer later.

If ushers are not in sight, the man leads the way down the aisle and stands aside for the woman to enter the pew before him. A man and woman may go down the aisle together with the woman entering the row first.

Remind your children before going into the sanctuary that the worship service is to be quiet and reverent. Instruct them to whisper if they must talk to you. Some parents teach their children to use their "quiet voice."

The Parent's Responsibility. Stay in contact with your child's teacher or the director of your child's group. Ask what you can do to help. Get instructions or directions about specific projects. Church teachers volunteer their time and need all the assistance and appreciation we can give them.

You or your child, or each of you, should write a note of thanks at the end of the church year when promotion time comes. Thank the teachers for their time, effort, and for perhaps meeting some special need of your child. (Our hyperactive child kept all his teachers active trying to keep up with him and trying to keep him down. We remember his teachers, and we are still grateful.) Don't be too concerned about the notepaper, form, or punctuation of your note. The recipients will appreciate the thought. If you keep a supply of paper, a pen, an address book, and stamps in a drawer or a convenient nook, you will send more notes and enjoy writing them.

The Pastor, Preacher, Reverend, Father, Rabbi. What do you call the minister in a particular church? It is not correct to use the term Reverend or the Reverend alone when speaking to or about a church dignitary. We must say Pastor, Rabbi, Dean, Dr., Father (or other title) before the last name. Mr. Swaryzmarth is always correct if you cannot be more specific.

Politeness

Politeness requires that we address a member of the clergy by title. Unless we are very close friends, we do not assume a clergyman's first name. Sometimes members of the clergy ask us to use their first name. Mr. or Ms. is always appropriate if we are unsure about the proper title.

Always write "The" before Reverend when addressing an envelope: "The Reverend Swartzmarth." "The Reverend Dr. Sam Tate and Mrs. Tate." To address a piece of correspondence going only to Dr. Tate, write: "The Reverend Sam Tate, D.D.," followed by the address on the next line.

If you are writing a female member of the clergy and her husband, address the envelope: "The Reverend Dr. Anne Masters and Mr. Robert Masters," followed by the address on the next line.

What about addressing an envelope to a priest? If he is a monsignor, write: "The Right Reverend Monsignor Patrick McKeller," followed by the address on the next line. In the letter write "Dear Monsignor McKeller."

If he is a priest but not a monsignor, address the envelope: "The Reverend Father Patrick McKeller," followed by the address on the next line. In the letter write "Dear Father McKeller."

What about a nun? If you know her order, write the initials after her name: "Sister Felicia Lowery, RSCJ," followed by the convent on the next line and the address on the following line. She is greeted in person and in correspondence as "Sister Lowery."

What about addressing an envelope to a rabbi? If he has a scholastic degree, write: "Rabbi David Levin, D.D., L.L.D." (or whatever the title), followed by the address on the next line. In the letter write "Dear Rabbi Levin." Without such a degree, write: "Rabbi David Levin" on the envelope and "Dear Rabbi Levin" in the letter.

Participation

Participate in the recitation of creeds or beliefs that you feel comfortable joining. It is not necessary to kneel unless you wish to do so. However, you should stand with the congregation unless members are voting.

Participate in communion only if the minister invites everyone to take part and you wish to do so. While visitors are usually warmly greeted and appreciated, some groups expect only the members of that congregation to take part in the communion service. A Lutheran friend shared with me their congregational statement printed on the Sunday order of service paper. "We with love and spiritual care for God's people practice 'close communion.' This means as you come to the Lord's Supper you are affirming as members of the Lutheran Church Missouri Synod that Jesus Christ is your personal Lord and Savior."

Rather than take offense at that statement, we should honor their request. To criticize and call their belief "closed" communion, is bad manners and in poor taste.

Communion is an ordinance (or sacrament in some churches) of observing Jesus' death on the cross, His burial, and resurrection. Participants take a small wafer and a small glass of grape juice or wine from a common tray as it passes hand to hand down their pew. Believers hold them until the minister gives the instruction to eat and drink them to symbolize belief in Christ, and that He chose to be crucified for our sins, was buried, and was raised from the dead to live forever, taking believers to heaven when we die. When as believers we take part in communion (also called the Lord's Supper), we say with our actions that we believe He died for us as though we were the only one who ever sinned, needing His vicarious, sacrificial death. That is the reason it is usually only believers who take part in sharing the wafer and juice or wine.

In some churches members go forward, row by row, to kneel at the altar to observe holy communion. As a visiting family, you may remain seated when the others exit your pew.

Participate in the offering with a contribution, no matter how small. A plate or bowl of some kind is usually passed once during the service. Congregations of believers are self-supporting with no government funding.

The Quiet Way to Greet

Quietly introduce yourself when you welcome visitors in a service at your church. To make room for latecomers, move to the center of the pew. Repeat the name when you meet a newcomer. Offer your opened hymnal to a visitor. In some churches the members are asked to stand so they can recognize the seated visitors. Other churches reverse that custom. Ushers usually pass out cards for visitors to complete. The cards are placed in the offering plate as it is passed hand to hand down the pew.

The Purpose of the Focus

The purpose of any church service is to show reverence to God, worshiping Him in the company of others. Church is a good place to experience being in favor with God and man.

A Recipe for Sunday Morning Breakfast

Barbara and Dennis Rainey of Family Life Ministries are raising six children, getting them to church each Sunday. Here is a recipe that Barbara uses when she does not have time to cook a big breakfast.

Barbara Rainey's French Toast Recipe

The night before:

> Mix ½ cup margarine,
> 1½ cup brown sugar,
> 1 teaspoon cinnamon,
> 8 eggs,
> a pinch of salt, and
> 1¾ to 2 cups milk.

Place eight to twelve slices of bread in a baking dish and pour mixture over the bread. Cover and let stand overnight in the refrigerator. Sunday morning, bake it for 45 minutes in a 350-degree oven. Turn it out upside down onto a platter.

Serve with warm syrup to a family seated together, or let each member serve himself buffet style.

For a healthier version, use low-fat bread, an egg substitute, low-fat margarine, and 1 percent milk.

It is still delicious.

Appendix A

• • •

Handling Food
from A to Z

This appendix is for all those who carry some Perfecter traits or have an appetite for a serendipitous experience delving into some of the reasons behind the rules, the proper way to eat the nearly impossible, and sundry questions that students and readers have asked. Most reasons behind the rules are based on safety, hygiene, and pleasing behavior. Without sufficient room for every reason, I have sprinkled selected ones throughout the appendix.

Eating the Nearly Impossible from A to Z:

- Asparagus: By reputation, it is a finger food, but it is sometimes overcooked and limp as a noodle, forcing us to eat it with a fork.
- Avocado: When filled with salad, use a fork. When served in the shell with salad dressing, use a spoon.
- Bacon: When limp, eat it with a fork. When it is dry and crisp, you may use your fingers.
- Baked Potato: Make a slit in the top of the foil and garnish a small portion at a time with your fork. Don't stir up a gooey mess. Replenish garnishment as needed. When the butter and

sour cream are passed, put a dollop onto your plate, transferring it to your potato after you pass the dish to the person on your right.

- Bread or Rolls: Break off a small portion, buttering it over your plate. Finish eating it before you break off another piece. Don't hold flat bread in the flat palm of your hand while you butter it. Loaf bread served on a board is sliced with a knife. You may halve a biscuit or roll, butter it, and eat from that half.

- Caviar: Spread it on a cracker with a knife. Made from fish eggs, caviar is an expensive, salty relish.

- Celery, Olives, and Other Relishes: Typically, they are finger foods if no toothpick is provided. You may use a fork, but don't chase an olive around your plate, finally spearing the little escapee. Use a serving spoon or fork to retrieve items from a communal dish.

- Cherry Tomatoes: If not served in a salad, they are a finger food. In a salad, cut with a knife or leave them whole to eat. They do squirt if you bite into one, and a bad one can almost send us gagging to the rest room.

- Chicken (Fried): At picnics or fast-food restaurants, plastic forks and paper plates or boxes call for eating chicken with the fingers. Tablecloths usually mean that we should eat the chicken with a knife and fork. In someone's home, watch the hostess for your cue.

- Clams and Oysters: Spear one with the small shellfish fork (or the smallest fork provided). Eat them whole. When they are served as hors d'oeuvres, on a picnic, or in a clam and oyster bar, pick the shell up in your fingers and let the morsel slide into your mouth.

- Corn on the Cob: Because it is never served at formal meals, it may be eaten with the fingers. Butter and season a small portion at a time. Don't eat up and down the row like a "mowing machine."

- Crab Legs: A seafood cracking tool should be provided. After the claws are cracked, the shells are pulled apart with the fingers and the meat is pulled out with the small oyster fork. The meat is dipped into melted butter before eating. The small claws are pulled from the body with the fingers and then put in the mouth with the body end of the claws between the teeth so that the meat can be extracted by chewing. Be careful not to make a sucking noise as you chew on these tasty bits. If no crackers or implements are provided, use your hands. Soft-shell crabs are considered a great delicacy and are eaten with a knife and fork. You may wish to remove the black vein and lay it on the plate.

- Dips: Whether you are dipping chips or raw vegetables into a dip dish, transfer it to your buffet plate if you have one. If you have only a napkin, hold the napkin under it while you retreat from the communal bowl before placing the chip in your mouth. Never transfer it directly to your mouth from the communal bowl. We must never appear to be eating from the dip dish. Never take a bite from a chip or vegetable and then put it back in the dip mixture to dip it again. Never "fish" around for a submerged chip with your fingers. If fresh vegetables are passed at the table, place them on your bread plate, salad plate, or whatever plate you have. Never eat from the serving plate.

- Finger Bowls: You will sometimes sniff a fragrance or see flower petals floating. Lemon wedges are appropriate in finger bowls only after a lobster feast. If the waiter or hostess brings a finger bowl before dessert, place the spoon to the right and the fork to the left of your plate. Lift the finger bowl and its doily, placing them to the left of your place. The dessert will then be served on the plate. After everyone finishes with dessert, you will use the finger bowl as instructed in chapter 12. If the finger bowl arrives without utensils, you are to use it when everyone has a bowl. Believe it or not, during the nineteenth century the custom of rinsing out the mouth and spitting the water back into the finger bowl fell into disuse.[1]

- Fish: Eat baked fish with a fish knife and fish fork if they are available. The rules for fried chicken apply to fried fish.

- French-fried potatoes: The same rules for fried chicken apply.

- Garnishes: Parsley, dill, watercress, mint, and other garnishments may be eaten with the fork as part of the dish of food, if you wish.

- Grapefruit: Use a spoon, preferably a serrated one. Do not squeeze the juice into a spoon except at home.

- Gravy: Ladle gravy from the gravy boat. Don't pour it. If you like bread soaked in gravy, put a small piece of bread in the gravy on your plate and eat it with your fork. Long ago, that custom was called "sopping the gravy." People sopped with their fingers and did so only at home.

- Hors d'oeuvres: We often call hors d'oeuvres *appetizers*. The English translation of the French is "outside the works." They have not always been served first. Once they were side dishes.[2]

- Lemon and Fish: A lemon squeeze is a lemon wedge wrapped in cheese cloth to prevent squirting juice on someone when you squeeze your lemon. Without a lemon squeeze, use the same hand method you used with iced tea.
- Meat: Cut one bite at a time. Otherwise, the food will get cold quickly and the plate will look messy.
- Melons: Diced melons and cantaloupes are eaten with a spoon.
- Pickles: Served with a sandwich, pickles are eaten with the fingers. When served with meat, a fork is used.
- Pizza: It is informal food fare. Hold a slice with your fingers. Nibble. Don't stuff your mouth.
- Salad: You may cut the lettuce with your knife and fork. That was once a taboo. Before stainless steel was invented, a metal knife blade could not be used because the vinegar in the dressing would turn the knife black. Because the salad plate often disappears before the entrée comes, keep your knife by placing it on another plate, such as your bread plate. Never place used silverware back on the tablecloth.
- Salt and pepper: Always pass the shakers together. The saying goes: "Never divorce the salt and pepper." Set them on the table. Don't pass them from your hands to someone else's hands.
- Sandwiches: Cold sandwiches are eaten as finger food. Eat hot sandwiches in a plate with knife and fork.
- Shish Kebab: Hold the meat-filled spear in one hand and your fork in the other hand against the handle of the spear. As you pull the spear, push the food off with your fork onto your plate. Eat each piece with your fork, cutting it with your knife, if necessary,
- Shrimp Cocktail: In a tall seafood dish, do not cut the shrimp with a knife. Spearing it with your fork, you may bite into a large shrimp. Cutting it with the edge of your fork is preferable. You may use your left hand to hold the compote steady at the base of the stem. Shrimp cocktail is one of the few foods we can bite into while it is still on the fork.
- Sorbet: Served immediately before the entrée to cleanse the pallet, it is an icy mixture of frozen fruit juices. It never contains milk, as sherbet does. Milk coats the mouth.
- Sorbet:
  - 2 cups sugar
  - 2 cups water
  - 2 tablespoons graded lemon rind
  - ¾ cup lemon juice unstrained

Set the juice aside. Combine the other ingredients and heat to dissolve. Cool the mixture. Add lemon juice and freeze in small compotes or in an ice cube tray to dish up later. Allow sorbet to thaw slightly for easier eating.

For variations, use bananas, strawberries, or limes.

- Soup: Soup bowls, cups, and even soup plates should have a plate beneath them. Anytime you put the soup spoon down, always place it on the plate, not in the bowl or cup. When you have a large, shallow soup plate with a wide rim, you may place the spoon in it rather than on the plate beneath it. The soup spoon handle is low enough to thwart an accident, such as bumping the handle and flinging the spoon across the table.

- Spaghetti and Sauce: The proper way to eat pasta is to use your fork in your right hand to wind the spaghetti against the inside rim of your plate. Then quickly bringing the bite to your mouth, be careful not to slurp up leftover strands. Wind the spaghetti around the fork in the bowl of a large spoon only in very casual settings. (This is the only exception to the rule about placing a spoon in the right hand.) Follow the lead of your hostess.

- Stewed Fruit: Eat with a spoon. Unobtrusively deposit any pits into the spoon and back into your bowl.

- Tortillas: Tacos are eaten with the fingers. Soft tortillas are eaten with a fork.

- Toothpicks in hors d'oeuvres: Collect them in your paper napkin until you can find a wastebasket or a small plate near the hors d'oeuvres tray for the used picks. Never put them back on the serving platter. Never leave one in your mouth. Toothpicks in club sandwiches should be placed near the edge of your plate before eating the sandwich.

- Zucchini: Eat this vegetable with a fork. It is a green squash before it is peeled.

Appendix B

• • •

Do's and Don'ts

Below are some important do's and don'ts about food and dining. Positive statements are always better than negative ones when we are instructing others. My challenge to you as a parent is to rephrase the don'ts into positives. For instance, "Don't take a second bite with food in your mouth" can be changed to "Swallow one bite before taking another one."

You will no doubt agree that some faux pas are so bad they lose something when we couch them in positive terms. The first don't is a good example.

Some Important Do's

- Do choose only one or two pieces of a food from a dish unless directed otherwise, or unless there is a variety.
- Do peel and break or cut up whole fruit when you are seated at a table.
- Do remove a tea bag with your spoon and place it on the saucer beside the cup.
- Do spread jellies and jams with a knife, never a fork.
- Do eat sorbet with the small spoon brought with it. Place it on the plate (not in the sorbet dish) any time the spoon is not in your hand.
- Do eat seafood such as shrimp cocktail with the seafood fork at the far right of the place setting. It is the only fork you will ever see on the right side of your plate.
- Do pass containers with a handle(s) turned toward the intended receiver. Set heavy dishes on the table next to the person on your right or hold it for him to serve himself.
- Do pass dishes counterclockwise (to the right) after you serve yourself.[1] It is not necessary to offer a serving to the person on your right before serving yourself. After the initial pass once around the table, the dish is then passed in either direction, taking the shortest route to the person who needs another serving.
- Do ask the hostess for any item missing from your place setting. "Mrs. Hostess, I seem to be missing a fork."
- Do securely position your fork and knife across the plate when passing it for another serving.
- Do say, "Please pass the (dish)." If the dish is very close to you, you may serve yourself. If you do, offer to pass it to anyone who might need it.
- Do feel free after someone requests a dish near you to say, "You won't mind if I help myself first so that you won't have to send it back this way."
- Do put any item of food on your plate before eating it, for instance, a roll or a pickle. Put after-dinner mints on your napkin or in the palm of your other hand before popping one into your mouth (to avoid appearing to eat from the bowl).
- Do position the female guest of honor to the right of the host with the male guest of honor on the hostess's right.
- Do cover your mouth with your napkin for a sneeze or an urgent cough. Turn your head down and to one side. Avoid sneezing on your neighbor or any food. Afterwards, say, "Pardon me." Don't blow your nose at the table.

Some Important Don'ts

- Don't ever spit anything out of your mouth.
- Don't stuff your mouth with food.
- Don't reach across the table or in front of others.
- Don't meet your food halfway with a rhythmic "ducking" motion. Bring the food to your mouth, leaning forward only slightly.
- Don't cut up an entire portion of food, such as meat. Cut one or two bites at a time.
- Don't push your plate away after you finish eating.
- Don't announce any allergies or dislike for particular foods. You may discreetly inform the hostess of any allergies to food you may have so that she will know why you do not eat something she serves.
- Don't put your used utensil into any communal dish. For instance, don't put your fork into the relish dish, and don't put a wet spoon in the sugar bowl.
- Don't gesture with your silverware as you talk.
- Don't talk with food in your mouth.
- Don't talk about unappetizing or argumentative topics around food.
- Don't wear male headgear such as hats and ball caps indoors except in places such as gymnasiums and in certain religious places.
- Don't scratch, pull at your clothes, or pick your teeth.

Appendix C

• • •

Questions and Answers

I have condensed the following questions from my newspaper column:

Q. We always say the blessing in our home before every meal. Is it right to say grace when we have guests?

A. Definitely. Dinner guests will appreciate it. The person who is to say the blessing should explain, "We always say grace in our family. We would like to do that now," or a similar phrasing. Some families join hands with family members and guests while they pray. It is polite to announce your intentions to prevent embarrassing a guest.

Q. Is it ever permissible to put my elbows on the table?

A. Yes, but in America doing so is proper only when there is no food on the table. Europeans and most other cultures rest both forearms on the table while they eat. The reason? They hold their knife and fork at all times. We lay our knife down and change the fork to the right hand, resting our left arm in our lap as we eat the bite we have cut.

Q. What if I have to burp?

A. Cover your mouth with your napkin. Try to release the air with your mouth closed. Quietly say, "Pardon me" or "excuse me." Do not talk about the problem.

Q. What should I tell my child to do with her dental appliance at meals in public?

A. Tell her to remove it before approaching the table, putting it in a pocket or purse or self-container. If she must remove it at the table, tell her to hide her mouth with her napkin as she removes it. The danger of storing it in a napkin or tissue can be expensive. My young students tell me repulsive stories of searching through the garbage at school looking for a lost appliance.

Q. How do I signal with my silverware that I have finished eating?

A. Place the knife (cutting edge turned toward the user) and the fork parallel on the plate diagonally from upper left to lower right with the handles pointing to the right. Americans leave the tines of the fork turned upward. Others turn them downward. Make sure they will not fall off the plate when it is removed.

Q. What is Continental style eating?

A. The fork remains in the left hand with tines down after food is cut. The inverted fork carries the bite to the mouth. The knife may be used to push errant food such as peas onto the backside of the tines for easier conveyance; however, the knife is not raised to the mouth along with the fork.

Q. Why do we in the United States hold our knife and fork differently from all other countries?

A. In all my research in twenty-eight libraries, this reason for our etiquette rules has been the most elusive. We eat American style and others in the world eat Continental style.

According to *The Rituals of Dinner* by Margaret Visser, and other research, here is my answer.

The fork was introduced in Italy in the eleventh century, but its resemblance to the devil's pitchfork kept it out of use until 1361. Another two hundred years passed before forks were commonly used for eating.

As late as 1837 everyone still ate by putting food into their mouths with a rounded-blade knife held in the right hand. With tines down, the fork was held in the left hand simply to hold down the food while the knife did its work.

Forks did not come into wide acceptance until the 1800s. To elevate the status of the fork (and to set the well-to-do Europeans apart from the commoners), they began downplaying the importance of the knife by laying it down and putting the fork in the right hand to carry food to the mouth, which had been the knife's privilege for centuries.

By 1880 the English introduced yet another new fashion of keeping the knife in the right hand and lifting the food to the mouth with the fork held in the left hand. Maneuvering such a balancing act (taking food to the mouth on the back of the fork tines) was considered a triumph of practice and determination—another status symbol.

Forks came late to America where people still ate with a rounded-blade knife held in the right hand. After forks took on their modern spoon-like form, Americans began favoring the use of the fork over the knife for conveying food, but deeply entrenched in the old way of carrying food to the mouth with the right hand, they began laying down the knife and changing hands so the fork could do the honors, hence our zig-zag way of eating. We never adopted the new European custom of inverting the fork in the left hand to lift food to our mouths.

We were not the ones who changed. The Europeans were; that is, they changed from using their right hand to using their left hand to carry food to their mouths.

Q. How do I decline coffee, tea, or any other beverage including alcohol?

A. Simply say, "No, thank-you." You need not make any explanation whatsoever. If the server or others at the table protest and persist, remain assertive, but courteous. No one should ever insist that another diner eat or drink anything nor explain his or her choices.

It is not proper to cover the cup or glass with your hand or turn it upside down. The waiter should remove the empty vessel. A hostess will remember your, "No, thank-you."

Q. Must I eat everything offered at a dinner?

A. It is polite to take a little of everything and eat only what you can without comment. If someone insists, say, "I'm saving room for dessert."

Q. Should I eat everything on my plate or leave a little food?

A. Either way you are using proper dining etiquette; however, refrain from scraping the plate clean or heaping your plate with food you do not plan to eat.

Q. At a church supper or other large gathering, is it necessary to wait until everyone is served before beginning?

A. Usually, the invocation is first in order. After people begin getting their plates, they must wait until five or six people around them have food before beginning. It is not necessary to wait for everyone unless the table is small. You may say, "I'm sure we should begin before the food gets cold."

Q. How do I know which utensil to eat with, especially when there are some I do not even recognize?

A. The rule of thumb is to begin with the utensil that you see farthest from the plate and work your way inward as each course is served. If the first course is soup, the spoon will be to the extreme right of the plate. (If there is an iced teaspoon, it may be to the right of the soup spoon.) If the dessert pieces are on either side of the plate, the soup spoon may be at the top. Remember, the bowl of a soup spoon is usually larger and/or more rounded than dessert spoons.

Q. If a server approaches me with a platter of food and places a big serving spoon and fork on the table for me to use, what do I do?

A. Take the spoon in your right hand and the fork in your left. With the tines of the fork downward, place the fork on the top of the serving as you slide the spoon underneath. Lift the portion slowly, letting the gravy or juice finish dripping before transferring that portion to your plate. Place the used serving pieces securely on the platter with both fork and spoon turned downward. The server will then take the platter to the next person who serves himself the same way.

Q. Why is it important to place the folded edge of my dinner napkin toward my knees?

A. By reaching toward the knees to lift the napkin by the fold to our mouth, we use the front side of it to dab any food residue. When we replace the napkin in the same position in our lap, we will not get any food smudges from the napkin onto our dress or trousers.

Q. What do I do with my napkin when I finish and when I must leave the table temporarily.

A. In both cases, "with the soiled side hidden, place the napkin on the left side of your plate, or if the plates have been removed, [place it] in the center."[1] If you put your napkin in your chair, you may get food on your clothes when you return to your seat.

Q. What if I get something in my mouth I cannot swallow?

A. Cover your mouth with your napkin. Use whichever utensil is in your hand to take out the offending morsel and place the unsightly thing under something like the parsley on your plate.

In other words, take it out with whatever you used to put the bite into your mouth.

If you put it in your napkin, you may forget about it and drop in onto the floor when you lift your napkin. If you place it under the rim of your plate, it will stare at you when the plate is removed.

Q. Is it proper to apply makeup at the table?

A. Only lipstick may be applied, and preferably without a mirror. All other grooming repairs must be done away from the table. Women and men alike should refrain from touching their hair when food is present. (Business women must retreat to the ladies' room to apply any makeup whatsoever.)

Q. When should a man or woman rise from a dining or restaurant table?

A. Women do not rise from a table in social settings when someone approaches. When a woman leaves and returns to the table, her escort or the man nearest her rises. All the men at a small table rise when a woman stops to visit briefly. If a man is confined, he may attempt to rise slightly or nod his head as he speaks.

When the group is large and a male visitor approaches, only the men closest to the visitor rise and shake hands. If a man stops by the table to speak to only one man, that man rises, shakes hands, and visits briefly.

Q. In most social situations, why should a man allow a lady to present her hand for a handshake before extending his?

A. Long ago, men extended their open hand to other men to show they were a friend and not an enemy. Since women usually did not carry a weapon, they did not shake hands. Men kissed a lady's extended hand. It was her prerogative to offer it.

Q. What if I drop something onto the tablecloth or spill something?

A. With your knife blade or a clean spoon, retrieve a solid piece of food and place it on the edge of your plate. If it caused a stain or a mess, use your napkin to absorb any liquid, apologize to the hostess, and offer to help clean up in any way you can.

Q. My child is left-handed. Should I set the table differently for her?

A. We do a child a disservice if we rearrange a place setting to accommodate him or her because we live in a right-handed society. Throughout her life she will see only standard place settings. You must help her learn to cope while she is young. (I saw a most appropriate sign that read, "Lefties have rights, too.")

Q. Where does the phrase "mind your p's and q's" come from?

A. In any language that admonition means to be careful about what you say and do. One explanation I found reminds us that the letters "p" and "q" look the same except in the distinctive way each is turned. Long ago when type was set by hand, typesetters feared they might reverse the two letters; therefore, they were especially careful with the "p" and the "q." They did not want to offend the reader. We must be careful of the rules of etiquette so that we do not offend others.

Q. Do I dig in as soon as the food is served?

A. In a home watch the hostess for all cues. In a restaurant wait until everyone is served. At a banquet wait until those around you have been served.

Q. Can we eat any differently at home than in public?

Princess Grace of Monaco taught it well. At breakfast in a fine hotel she saw her children squeezing the juice from their grapefruit into a spoon to get the last drop. She discreetly taught them that there were a few differences in "at home manners" and "in public manners." She said they could squeeze their grapefruits at home. Another example might be crumbling crackers in your soup.

Q. *How many portions of a main dish should I take when the pieces are small?*

A. You may take two after you assess the approximate number in the dish and the number of people dining with you.

Q. *Why is it improper to refold a napkin?*

A. Presumably to indicate that it is soiled and not to be used by another. Long ago, diners replaced their linen napkin into a napkin ring and used it again at the next meal. (They obviously did not do laundry as often as we do.)

Q. *Why is it proper to pass food to the right?*

A. When we pass food to the right, we permit the recipient to take it with his left hand and serve himself with his right hand.

Appendix D

• • •

Recommended Resources

A Call to Family Reformation by Dennis Rainey, Family Life Ministries, A Ministry of Campus Crusade for Christ.

A Child's Book of Manners (Preschool Activity and Coloring Book), based on the book by Ruth Shannon Odor, Standard Publishing Company 1995.

Crane's Blue Book of Stationery by Steven L. Feinberg, Doubleday.

Do's and Taboos Around the World, edited by Roger Axtell, published by John Wiley & Sons, Inc.

Emily Post's Etiquette 15th Edition by Elizabeth Post, Harper Collins.

Family Life Marriage and Parenting Conferences. Call 1-800-358-6329

Manners Matter (workbook) by Debbie Pincus, Good Apple.

Personality Plus by Florence Littauer, Fleming Revell.

Understanding Why Others Misunderstand You, Ken Voges and Ron Braund, Moody Press.

Your Child's Hidden Needs by Dr. Bruce Narramore, Dean of Rosemead School of Psychology at Biola University. The book is published by Fleming Revell.

Endnotes

Chapter 1
1. The Moody Bible Institute, *The Wycliffe Bible Commentary* (Nashville, Tenn., The Southwestern Company, 1962), 1033.
2. *Arkansas Baptist News magazine.*

Chapter 2
1. Dr. T. Berry Brazelton, *Families Today*, February 18, 1996.
2. *The Charles Ryrie Study Bible,* NAS, 968.

Chapter 3
1. Carol McD. Wallace, "Minding Kids' Manners," *Redbook*, August 1994, 146.
2. Elizabeth Post, *Good Housekeeping*, June 1994.
3. Letitia Baldrige, Manners for the '90s, Rawson Associates, N.Y., N.Y., 1990, 37.

Chapter 4
1. U.S. Department of Education Office of Educational Research and Improvement, "Helping Your Child Learn Responsible Behavior," Series of booklets, 1993.

Chapter 6
1. *Parents*, 1989, 33.

Chapter 13
1. Paula M. Siegel, *Good Housekeeping*, Jan. 1996, 69.

Chapter 14
1. Clare Collins, "New York Opera Series Teaches Children How to Appreciate Performing Arts," *New York Times News Service. Arkansas Democrat Gazette*
2. Ibid., 3.
3. Nicole Brodeur, "To Dismay of Film Fans, Theaters Full of Rude People," *Orange Co. Register.*

Appendix A
1. Margaret Visser, *The Rituals of Dinner* (New York: Grove Weidenfeld, 1991).
2. Ibid.

Appendix B
1. Elizabeth Post, *Etiquette*, 15th ed., (New York: Harper Collins Publishers, 1992), 108.